MY LIFE AND SPIRITUAL JOURNEY

MY LIFE AND SPIRITUAL JOURNEY:

From Tragedy to Acceptance, How One Atheist Looked Beyond Doctrines To Integrate Our World's Religions

Marshall L. Shearer, MD

Fresh Ink Group

Roanoke

MY LIFE AND SPIRITUAL JOURNEY:
From Tragedy to Acceptance, How One Atheist Looked Beyond Doctrines To Integrate Our World's Religions

Copyright © 2011
Marshall L. Shearer, MD

Fresh Ink Group
An Imprint of:
The Fresh Ink Group, LLC
PO Box 525
Roanoke, TX 76262
Email: info@FreshInkGroup.com
www.FreshInkGroup.com

Edition 1.0   2011
Version 1.1   2011

Book design by Ann E. Stewart

Cover design by Joe Posada

Cataloging-in-Publication Recommendations: Non-Fiction; Autobiography; Memoir; Spirituality (Biography); Religion (Biography); Religious Studies (Biography); Atheism (Biography); Psychiatry (Biography); Relationship Expert (Biography); Author (Biography)

Library of Congress Control Number: 2010940802

ISBN-13: 978-1-936442-02-7

To all of us who are
following our own spiritual paths.

Are you on the journey you desire?
Are you satisfied with your progress?
You may benefit from the wisdom of one or more gurus.
I have found many as friends, at lectures, or in books.
Ask others for recommendations.
Be persistent.
Keep searching until you find and follow your path.

Table of Contents

Who I am and how I came to write this book

A Brief Overview

My name is Marshall Shearer, M.D. I am 77 years old (2010). My wife, Peggy, and I have been married for 48 years, the only marriage for either of us. We have three adult children of whom we are very proud. We lost a premature infant who lived only twenty-two hours.

I went through medical school with the goal of becoming a general practitioner. During my internship, I decided to become a psychiatrist; the human need seemed greater. During my psychiatric training at the University of Michigan, I met Peggy, who was a senior medical student. Including my residencies in psychiatry and in child psychiatry, and as an instructor and associate professor, I was at the University of Michigan for eleven years. In 1970, Peggy and I joined the staff of the Masters and Johnson Institute as clinical and research associates in St. Louis, Missouri. In 1972, we returned to Michigan. Peggy went into family medicine and later administrative medicine. I opened a private practice in psychiatry and served as a Clinical Associate Professor at the University of Michigan. Together we wrote a "sex help" column for the *Detroit Free Press* one to three times a week, which was distributed over the Knight-Ridder wire service. This ended in 1996 after twenty-three years.

In September 1996, I was warned that I was facing cardiac surgery. I was advised to reduce stress and take off weight. I was able to close my practice in an orderly manner. In March 1997, I had five coronary bypasses and my aortic heart valve replaced with a graphite one. Following surgery, I had a shower of emboli-strokes to the frontal and temporal lobes of my brain. As a result, I was mentally "out of it"—that is, crazy though not psychotic for almost two years.

When I judged myself well enough to be able to carry on a conversation without grossly embarrassing myself, Peggy and I explored the Unitarian Universalist Church. I had heard of Reverend Ken Phifer and his church from two patients separately. After two months we joined the church.

I have not fully recovered, but I am functioning.

Spiritual Path

This writing contains a description of my spiritual path, how my religious questions arose, and how I dealt with them. My answers were and are satisfactory to me. When I reached my mid-sixties, I questioned whether my earlier answers would hold up to more intense scrutiny. In an effort to re-evaluate the principles I think I have lived by, and perhaps to aid others in their search, I started this project. Currently, it consists of two manuscripts: *Toward Interfaith Harmony* and this book, *My Life and Spiritual Path*.

Poems

Poetry has always been meaningful to me. It probably started with nursery rhymes. Later, I could recite Clement Moore's "A Visit From St. Nicholas," better known as "'Twas The Night Before Christmas." Throughout my life certain poems have spoken to me deeply. I will cite some of these in the appropriate context of this writing. The first of these, appropriate to the introduction, is *Abou Ben Adhem*[1] by James Henry Leigh Hunt. I thought of this poem as Arabic or Muslim in spite of the author's name. I am sure this influenced my later attitude. Since I first read this poem, it has expressed my philosophy for life as well as my religious attitude.

Abou Ben Adhem
By James Henry Leigh Hunt

Abou Ben Adhem (may his tribe increase!)
Awoke one night from a deep dream of peace,
And saw, within the moonlight in his room,
    Making it rich, and like a lily in bloom,
An Angel writing in a book of gold:
Exceeding peace had made Ben Adhem bold,
And to the Presence in the room he said,
"What writest thou?" The Vision raised its head,
And with a look made of all sweet accord
Answered, "The names of those who love the Lord."
"And is mine one?" said Abou. "Nay, not so,"
Replied the Angel. Abou spoke more low,
But cheerly still; and said, "I pray thee, then,
Write me as one that loves his fellow-men."

The Angel wrote, and vanished. The next night
It came again with a great wakening light,
And showed the names whom love of God had blessed,
And, lo! Ben Adhem's name led all the rest!

Family History

Three lines of our family tree consisted of a Baptist minister about every other generation. My parents were quite religious Southern Baptists. My mother's father, Marshall Orlando Carpenter, was a professor of Old Testament and Greek; he also did some congregational preaching. For more than two decades, he had been a Home Missionary in southern Georgia. He and his wife, Claudia Elizabeth Waff Carpenter, had two daughters.

Among his many jobs, my paternal grandfather served as sheriff, ran a hardware store, and for several years was a wheat rancher in Alberta, Canada. He was one of the oil producers bankrupted by John D. Rockefeller's policy of lowering the price of crude oil to force other producers out of business. He and my grandmother had five boys and two girls who survived past infancy. He was a hard, no-nonsense man who was quick to punish.

One story is emblematic of his harshness. When my father was learning his multiplication tables, his father asked him what four times eight was. Dad missed the answer. His father hit him in the mouth, knocking Dad off his stool and saying, "Four times eight is 32, and don't you ever forget it." His younger two children received fewer whippings than those born earlier. They did not develop inferiority complexes.

My parents met when my father's sister, Ottie, took my mother to her family's home one college vacation.

As a teenager, my father had two nicknames: "the boy preacher" and "the bull." He was quick to fight. Dad earned a master's degree from Harvard in Kinesiology, a branch of physical education. Mother received her bachelor's degree in 1922 from Peabody State Teacher's College in the same graduation ceremony that awarded her father his master's degree. He became the first faculty member hired at a new college, Bluefield College, in West Virginia. The college provided housing; his was No. 1 Faculty Row.

Both of my parents had considered becoming missionaries, but didn't. They married June 5, 1928.

My mother coached women's basketball. My father was a football coach, a quite colorful football coach. News of my mother's first pregnancy generated excitement in the community. Mother went into labor around midnight. The doctor had been short of sleep, attending to other patients. He gave mother something to slow labor to enable him to get some rest. Dad said he put his ear to Mother's abdomen and heard a strong, steady heartbeat. My brother was born dead about six hours later. Both of my parents blamed the medication. There was no talk of being punished by God. Reportedly, they asked the doctor how long they should wait before trying again. The answer was five to six months. I was born fourteen months later—at home, to avoid losing me as they had my brother.

Mother said that I had eye infections right after birth, and that she would have to take a warm washcloth to bathe my eyes so I could open them.

Parental Love

My mother and grandmother read and told me *Bible* stories. I had age-appropriate religious books with pictures.

I am not sure of the dates of the next three stories, nor of the sequence.

My maternal grandfather had two remarkable personality traits: he never got angry, and he was a terrible tease. I have felt these two traits were different expressions of the same trait. My mother said he would sometimes tease his wife to the point of tears. As one Christmas approached when I was three or four years old, he began teasing me that he was going to shoot Santa. He had me in tears. My mother said he didn't mean it, and that he would not shoot Santa, but no one told him to stop. I don't think my father was present. I believe he would have protected me; further, I doubt my grandfather would tease me to that extent if Dad had been present. This teasing was from a representative of

God of Love, the same God who said, "Suffer the little children to come unto me for such is the kingdom of heaven."

I had similar objections to the story in one of my books of Abraham almost sacrificing his son Isaac to God. In Genesis 22:2-14, an angel of the Lord told Abraham to take his son Isaac to "a place that I will show you and make a burnt sacrifice of him." Abraham took wood and his son to the place God told him. Isaac asked his father where the animal was that was to be sacrificed. Abraham said, "The Lord will provide." Abraham bound Isaac and laid him on the wood, which was on top of the altar. Then Abraham took his knife to slay his son, but an angel stopped him. The angel said, "Do not do anything to the lad for now I know that you fear God, seeing you have not withheld your only son from God." The Muslims believe that it was Ishmael, Isaac's older half brother by Abraham, who was about to be sacrificed.

I cannot accept this story. Again, this is the God of love and justice. Second, God is omniscient—he knows everything before it happens. Jesus foretells Judas' betrayal of him. (Matthew 26:23) Further, Luke 12:7 says that "even the hairs on your head are numbered," and Luke 12:5 says, "I shall forewarn you whom you should fear." So God should know what the results of such a test would be without having to carry it out. Why would Abraham side with God against his son? Can this really be God talking? Would the God of Love and Justice ask such an act? Is the God who would ask such a thing worthy of love and worship? Even as the story is told, it is between God and Abraham. What about the effects on Isaac? He was well aware of his father's intent to sacrifice him.

It is the responsibility of every parent to love, protect, and nurture each child. For a child to get a message from his father— that his father is seriously considering getting rid of the child—

leaves lifetime scars. I know; I would experience a similar thought, which I talk about in the upcoming section titled "Dad Returns."

We spent the night one Christmas Eve at my grandparents' home. I hung my stocking on the mantelpiece. The next morning I came downstairs and saw my stocking with switches sticking out the top. I ran back upstairs crying. Santa brings presents to good boys and girls; he brings ashes and switches to bad boys and girls! I overheard my parents discussing what to do. Dad said, "Leave him alone; he will be back." Mother wanted to come to me. After an hour or two, Mother did come up. When she learned of my misperception, she said they were not switches; they were sparklers. She went downstairs, got my stocking, and brought it upstairs to me. She dumped the contents out on the bed. There were oranges like those my grandmother and I had eaten together. I accused Mother of replacing the switches and ashes from Santa with oranges, nuts, candy, and sparklers that she had. She denied it. I knew without a doubt that those oranges were put there by my family members. By this time, Dad had come upstairs. The issue sort of died there. I felt loved by my parents, even though condemned by Santa.

Eye Difficulty Detected

At age four, I was in the upstairs hall, in front of a sunlit window, when Dad asked me to cover my left eye and tell him what I saw. I was surprised that all I could see was a gray silhouette of his form. At age 6 the diagnosis of a detached retina in my right eye was made. For years afterwards Dad would ask me to cover my good eye and tell him how many fingers he held up. However, he always told me the correct answer. If the correct answer was two, then next time it would not be two, one, or three (the numbers on either side). This brought the odds from one in five to one in two. It pleased him when I got several in a row correct. I recall once he ran to Mother and announced, "Mildred, Mildred, he can see. He can see."

Mother quickly burst his bubble, explaining how I had learned to guess his pattern. That realization left Dad dejected. We didn't play that game after that. Of course, for Dad it was never a game—not consciously, at any rate.

"Baby Seeds"

Two of my maternal grandmother's brothers, Thomas and Joseph Waff, had taken up residence in Florida. They raised citrus fruit. They sent my grandmother a crate of fruit every Christmas. She and I would sit together. She would use a paring knife to peel oranges, which we would eat while we talked and she would tell me *Bible* stories. I felt close to her and loved her very much. My paternal grandmother died before I was born.

It was probably while my mother was pregnant with my brother that I asked where babies come from. Dad said, "Babies come from a seed that Dad puts in Mother's stomach." One day while eating an orange with my grandmother, I asked her what an orange seed was. She told me, including that an orange tree would grow from it. When I expressed skepticism, she reached over and poked a hole in the dirt at the edge of a flower pot, poked the seed in, and packed dirt over it. Much to my surprise, several weeks later a green shoot grew where she had planted the seed. Stomach was stomach, I thought, completely unaware that "stomach" was also a euphemism for uterus. I was afraid that if I swallowed an orange seed, I would have an orange tree growing in my stomach with branches coming out of every orifice of my head! After some days or weeks, I thought I could avoid orange seeds. But grape seeds remained a major threat.

Prayer Time

My grandfather would conduct family prayers whenever we stayed the evenings with them. I suspect it was primarily Saturday evenings that we were there. These prayers dragged on and on. They seemed interminable, especially to a young boy. He asked for God's blessing for each family member by name, then moved on to his list of relatives. Next came friends, followed by people in authority, e.g.: President Roosevelt and other officials. It was as though if he missed one something bad might happen to him or her.

I was critical of the prayers for their length; later I began to question their necessity and even their helpfulness. God knew the situations of everyone. He knew those who loved him. Did God bless those people who believed in Jesus, who were good and righteous, or did He bless those who were named in the most prayer petitions—or was it some combination? If so, how did God decide? If God knew everyone's needs, then why should grandfather need to ask? These questions may well have been my first serious questioning of the theology I was taught.

In 1937, the students dedicated the college annual, *The Rambler*, to my grandfather. He retired in June 1940.

Dad's Coaching Career

Dad had several jobs coaching football, including at Bluefield College for the 1936-37 school year. It was a colorful year. Dad was well liked. The team performed well that year. The college's contract with Dad specified that if he could get the football team out of the red financially that year, they would pay him an extra $1,000. He did. However, the Board of Trustees reasoned that if the payments on capital improvements to the football field were added in, even though this expense had never been part of the operating budget, then the college would not be obligated for the bonus. Dad felt they had been dishonest, and he refused to continue coaching on principle.

For the 1937-38 school year, Dad took a job coaching at Graham High School in Bluefield, Virginia. He took the team to Mill Springs, Kentucky, on Lake Cumberland, for a football camp. It had been built under the CCC (Civilian Conservation Corps) program. The camp burned about two months after the team left. Here I was introduced to rowing a boat—sitting "backwards."

Brother Bill and Questions

Mother delivered my brother six days after my 4th birthday on March 7, 1937. When he was just a few days old, there was a heavy snow, and for some reason Mother wanted to drive to her parents' home. She gave me the responsibility of sitting on the edge of the front seat with my infant brother behind me and of not letting him fall off. I have a vivid memory of the tension in the car, sitting on the seat, grasping the dashboard in front of me, watching the snowflakes against the windshield. We arrived safely.

That summer, my family visited my grandfather's relatives in Lincoln County, North Carolina. One morning, my grandfather asked to talk with my father. Mother was downstairs helping their hostess with the breakfast dishes. My parents had left my brother unattended in the middle of a double bed to take a nap, thinking he couldn't roll over. He did roll over and over and over—to the foot of the bed. He got a spindle of the bedstead across his windpipe. Efforts to revive him failed. I was playing in the dirt in front of the tractor shed when the cries of alarm went up at the discovery of his body.

I remember the graveside service quite vividly. I remember the man at the end of the first row in a blue shirt half soaked with sweat in the August sun, singing with the others, "On Jordan's

Stormy Banks I Stand." "Oh, who will come and go with me? I am bound for the Promised Land." I heard many comments that my brother was in heaven with God and that God took him, and that it was God's will. Dad would say years later that the tragic death of my baby brother was the one thing he never got over.

Over the next three years, I presented my mother with a number of questions about my baby brother's death, starting with, "Where is he now?" I had seen him in the casket and seen the casket lowered into the ground and covered with dirt. Southern Baptists don't believe in infant baptism. A person has to be old enough to think for himself. This was generally taken to be age ten to thirteen. Mother had characterized God to me as good, kind, just, and omnipotent, one who has a vested interest in the welfare of humans, *at least those who worship Him.* I had learned that the purpose of life was to live in ways that would result in getting into heaven. This required believing in Jesus. Mother said my brother was in heaven even though he was not old enough to believe in Jesus. He was in heaven because he had not had the opportunity to sin. I continued to ask many questions of my mother over the next three years.

My father was superintendent of Sunday schools at church. Mother and I frequently attended the church service. One Sunday, I wanted to see if Mother closed her eyes during prayer. To do so I had to get down so I could look up into her face. I had just gotten myself into position when Mother grabbed my shoulder with a firm squeeze. She also opened one eye closest to me and gave me a stare that was the "ultimate evil eye."

Sometime before we moved from Bluefield, Virginia, to Norfolk, Virginia, when I was seven, I had asked Mother, "If the purpose of life on earth is to get to heaven, and if you get to heaven when you die as an infant, then why didn't you kill me?" She replied, "Don't be ridiculous." I thought, but did not say, *It is not I who is ridiculous; it is your religion.* This ended my discussions with her about my brother's death.

On reflection years after that discussion, I realized she had dismissed the question as not serious. In so doing she swept aside, as "not worthy of consideration," all the theology she had been teaching me. I also realized that there were two or three answers that might have preserved her theology.

> One would be: "Where would that have left me? There is a Commandment, 'Thou shall not kill'," of which I was well aware. Later, I extended this thinking to a mother animal saving the life of her young at the cost of her own life. Wasn't eternal salvation more important than saving an earthly life? And Mother knew her theology. She would have known how to be forgiven for such an unselfish and loving act. Years would pass before I realized, "One doesn't play games with God."
>
> The second possible answer is included in the above paragraph, namely, "One doesn't manipulate God. He sees through it all."
>
> A third answer might have been, "That would have been choosing for you. It would not have been your choice and responsibility for how you live your life." Such an answer would tie back into one of the statements in the syllogism I presented to her in my question—the purpose of life on earth.

Long term, this left me with two persistent questions: How were the people who lived before Jesus' time supposed to be saved? And, How are the people who never heard of Jesus supposed to be saved? Neither group would have the opportunity to believe in Jesus. Mother's answers were unsatisfactory: "Those who lived before Jesus would be saved if they believed in the coming of the Messiah," and "The Great Commission was Jesus' command to go into all the world and preach the gospel so all people could be saved."

I recognized and articulated the unfairness of these positions, especially in regard to every infant's death. This was more than the "problem of evil"; it was a problem of fundamental fairness by an all-powerful, benevolent God who cared about humans and supposedly intervened in the world on their behalf. He/She/It was represented as being worthy of worship.

John 3:13-18

As a questioning teen, I received from Mother a set of books, including *An Interpretation of the English Bible* by Reverend B. H. Carroll.[2] Dr. Carroll takes as his starting point the prayers of Jesus as he approached the cross and was crucified. Jesus had prayed that this cup might be passed from him. Since it wasn't, Jesus concluded there was no other way. I can accept that in regard to Jesus and his mission, but not in the absolute sense. If God is fair and just, He would not condemn to hell all those who never heard of Him. I believe the other way without supernatural sanctions is in living a loving, compassionate life, believing in the personification of love. This standard could apply to all people everywhere. (See the poem "Abou Ben Adhem", which I quoted earlier.)

Another questionable objection for me has been the story of Judas. It is true that Jesus considered him a betrayer. Jesus came to die on the cross; that was his mission. The Romans wanted to be sure they had the right man, and Judas made that identification. In the broad picture, Judas furthered Jesus' mission, perhaps by a day. As I read this part of the *Bible*, I see Judas creating a confrontation between Jesus and the Roman authorities—to usher in Jesus' kingdom on earth. However, when Judas realized he had misunderstood Jesus, he hanged himself. I have expanded on this in "Concern About Fairness to Judas Iscariot." (See Exhibit A.)

The *Bible* story of Abraham almost killing Isaac as a sacrifice was disturbing to me. So, too, was the fact that he followed his wife's wishes by sending Ishmael and his mother into the desert, presumably to die. Couldn't Abraham stand up to her? After all, Sarah had suggested that Abraham sleep with her handmaiden, Hagar, to have a child.

Sallie's Birth, Bluefield, Virginia

When I was six, my sister Sallie was born July 22, 1939. Mother delivered Sallie at home, also. I was playing at a friend's house when the hostess came and told me that I had a baby sister. I was hurt. Why hadn't I been called to the phone to be told by Mother or Dad? I replied, "I know." Of course, I didn't know, but this lie restored the right priority of relationships. The fact that I had lied bothered me considerably.

Fastest Draw In All These Parts

My parents would not allow me to have a toy gun. In playing with my friends, I would slap my hip and come up with a pointed finger as a gun. As a result, I had the fastest draw in the neighborhood. My friends went to my parents, asking them to let me have a toy gun. They said it was unfair, that there was no way any of them could compete with me and my finger. My parents realized I was already "shooting" at others as much as if I had a toy pistol, and that their prohibition was hurting my peer relations. I got a toy pistol.

The Barksdale House

My family moved from the Steel house (landlord's name) to the first home my parents purchased, the Barksdale house. This property included three vacant lots. My sister Sallie wasn't doing well with whatever they were feeding her, so Dad bought two goats to supply her with milk. Dad gave me the job of milking them each morning, and paid me for the milk. This had the effect of my being respectful of the goats and protecting them from my playmates. Mother would come out each morning and take the goat milk from me and give me a wet towel for my hands before I caught the city bus to kindergarten.

My family also raised chickens for sale. We would get one-hundred baby chicks and put them in an incubator. Of every one-hundred chicks, three to six would die. It was my job to pick up the chicks that died and put the bodies in the furnace. When the chicks reached pullet size, Dad and Mother would butcher them, including picking all the feathers off. I sometimes helped with that part. Dad often cut the chickens up. Then he would drive, and I would take the chickens or eggs to the doors of customers. I did not get paid for the work with chickens. That was part of "home membership."

In 1939, Dad got a job as head of the 1940 census for the western part of the State of Virginia. This took him away from home for stretches at a time.

Moving to Norfolk

Dad was in charge of a Naval Reserve Communications Unit in Bluefield. He volunteered for active duty to begin January 1,

1940. He was assigned to the personnel office of the 5th Naval District in Norfolk, Virginia. Our move from Bluefield to Norfolk was delayed till July so Mother could sell the house while it was still occupied. The first grade started in Bluefield at age seven, presumably to cut down unemployment for a year after high school, but in Norfolk it started at age six. My parents wanted me to be with my age mates in Norfolk, so I had had some tutoring in Bluefield.

As we were driving out of Bluefield, a number of Dad's football players appeared in the road, holding hands, blocking the road. Dad got out of the car, and they exchanged goodbyes.

Norfolk

When I was seven, my family arrived in the Norfolk area in the summer of 1940. At Virginia Beach Dad had rented a second-floor apartment with a large concrete slab on the ground for a driveway and apron to the garages. Previous tenants had left a small tricycle—too small for me and too large for my one-year-old sister. I would put her on the seat and put one foot on the back of the bike and my hands on the handlebars, then push us around like a scooter. The cotter key had been lost from the left rear wheel. It was held in place by a bent nail. After I scraped my ankle on that nail, my ankle became infected. My whole leg became swollen—so swollen that I couldn't bend my leg. Dad took me to the Navy doctors. I overheard part of the conversation between the doctor and Dad. "The infection has progressed too far to try to remove the leg, but there is a new drug that might save him. The drug has not been released for public use. It is restricted for military use."

Dad asked, "Can we get some?"

The doctor replied, "For this, we can."

I realized they were talking about my life. I don't recall being anxious. I realized both of them cared about me and that they were doing all they could. I also knew there was nothing I could do.

The doctor did an incision and drainage. Six cups of pus were removed, and the new sulfa drug was put directly into the wound, as well as administered orally. To be near the Navy doctors, my family moved into the home of Mother's second cousin Edna Gray; her husband, Bill; and their high-school daughters, Mary Love and Margaret.

Blood poisoning was the real danger. There were several days in which I was not expected to survive. For my parents, that would have been three sons and three deaths.

My family moved into our own home shortly after my recovery. My parents had insisted on a home with two bedrooms on the first floor, one for each of my mother's parents. The house was on a peninsula, Edgewater, in Norfolk. There was a very wide cove on the Elizabeth River. The water was two short blocks away. In season, Dad and I could catch a bushel of crabs in an hour. Later, I would go crabbing alone. My parents joined the Larchmont Baptist Church, which had an active youth program.

My parents put me in a private school on the naval base for the second grade, a one-room with about twenty students in grades two through seven. I am not sure why they did, perhaps in hope for special help to compensate for me skipping the first grade. I continued there for two years.

We had friendly neighbors. Mr. Flynn owned a rowboat. Dad and I went out in the bay with him at least once. Then Dad or I could take the boat out any time as long as I wore a life vest.

Robert's Birth, Norfolk, Virginia

When I was eight, my brother, Robert Carpenter, was born May 22, 1941. The doctor had told my mother that he would not be her obstetrician unless she consented to deliver in the hospital. Mother agreed, but she concealed the progress of her labor from the nurses. She delivered in the labor room. Dad bought another milk goat, but I had lost the technique of milking, so the goat was sold.

Public School

By the fall of 1942 when I was nine, my parents realized I was not learning in the naval-base school. For the fourth grade, they moved me to public school, a mile and a block from home. During the first weeks, the boys in my class would clasp hands, run at me, and knock me down, then step on me. I told Dad about this. He asked if I knew who the ringleader was. When I said, "Yes," he told me to wait to the last second, throw myself on the ground, then roll under the ringleader's feet to knock the leader down, then jump up quickly and kick him. I did, but perhaps with too much force and vigor. It stopped the hazing, but I was partially shunned.

Preparing to Ship Out

Dad was in the personnel office of the 5th Naval District. He realized that the task of securing personnel for the war was winding down, so he began preparing to go overseas. He requested a combat assignment. In preparation, Dad had a new furnace put in the house. It had a screw mechanism to deliver coal from the coal bin directly into the firebox of the furnace. The only human attention required was removing the clinkers once a week. He trained me for that. He also purchased and installed an automatic washing machine. To do so, he went under the house and built up a brick and concrete foundation to anchor the washer. I held the extension-light cord for him.

Mother's Helper

Mother had an African-American woman come to help around the home once a week, which also enabled her to go shopping. Sometimes the helper brought her five-year-old son. He and Sallie played well together.

Jane's Birth, Norfolk, Virginia

Seven weeks before my tenth birthday, my sister Jane was born January 11, 1943. Mother had the same doctor, same hospital, and same determination. Again, she delivered in the labor room, in spite of the note in her chart about her prior delivery. She was avoiding the risk of being medicated to slow labor and perhaps kill the fetus. She was protecting her babies.

Grandfather's Heart Attack

My grandfather worried about the war in Europe a great deal. There had been sightings of German submarines off our eastern coast. There was concern of an air raid on Norfolk, "the back door to Washington, D.C." On a hot August night when I was ten, there was an air-raid drill. During that drill, my grandfather suffered a heart attack.

Through the open kitchen window, the air-raid warden called, "Lights out! This is an air raid!" My mother replied, "My father is having a heart attack, and I need to be able to see to fix him a hypodermic!" The warden said, "This is only a drill. Have all the light you need." (I get choked up every time I think of this.)

Crying, my mother called her sister, who came across town, air raid or not, to sit on the side of their father's bed. She sang to him in a clear and steady voice. "When the roll is called up yonder, I'll be there." My aunt didn't miss a note. It sounded beautiful, a memory that stays with me. Presumably, my grandfather died during that song.

He died in August 1943. My father left for overseas later in August, and my uncle was ordered to Boston in September. My mother's sister went with him. Quite a loss of support for Mother! I was ten years old; Sallie was six; Robert, two; and Jane, nine months.

My Grandmother, Mother, and Me

In October or November of 1943, I came home from school one day and called my mother, but there was no answer. That was unusual. Not to answer when called was a major "no-no." At length, I found her in the upstairs bathroom washing some things out in the sink. She was crying. When I spoke to her, she delayed answering me. At length, she asked me if I had taken $25 my grandmother had put in an envelope and set on her nightstand to give to the church. I told her I hadn't. She said that was like stealing from the church. I assured her I had not taken the money. She didn't believe me.

A sort of cold war developed between my mother and me. The highlight every week for my grandmother was to go for a car ride. The back of my grandmother's seat was jostled several times in a twenty-minute ride. I always got the blame because Grandmother would often call my name. Mother would think Grandmother had seen me. As a result, I was excluded from the family car rides. That was okay with me. Mother had the lowest priority card for gas rationing, but the only other gas we used was to get groceries once a week.

When Christmas came, Mother made sure I had a present for my grandmother. I wrapped a hard ash cinder in Christmas paper and put it under the tree. Mother was pleased, but when she saw it she was mad. I don't recall my punishment. Although Mother tolerated me, she treated me coldly.

Still only ten years old, I asked Mother if I could ride my bike to North Carolina to stay with our relatives, whom I had just seen at my grandfather's funeral. This was a desperate cry for help, especially the bike part! It was a 252-mile trip. Ideally, she could make the call and the arrangements; I wouldn't be running away. She might even arrange for my transportation. She could tell our relatives whatever she felt was necessary. It would be her finesse, not mine. I was sure she wanted me away from home almost as much as I. Mother didn't turn it down flat. She said she would write and ask Dad. I wasn't hopeful. At length, Dad wrote back: "I have already lost one son in North Carolina; I'm not going to risk another. The answer is 'no.'"

In the summer of 1944 when I was eleven, it was my aunt's turn to keep my grandmother for a year or two. My aunt was still in Boston. The idea was hatched for me to escort my grandmother on the train from Norfolk to Boston, changing trains in New York City. Traveler's Aid would meet us in New York City to be sure we caught the correct train. I saw it as a major relief. My aunt and I had always gotten along, and the prospect of not living in the same household with my mother and my grandmother for two years was delightful. I was all for it. It came to pass, and everything went smoothly. I was to return to Norfolk in time for school. Only as I write this some sixty-six years later do I recognize any connection between my proposed North Carolina trip and this trip to Boston.

Dad was still concerned and curious about my eye(s). A shipmate of his somewhere in the Pacific recommended that a particular Boston ophthalmologist see me. Dad wrote my aunt, and an appointment was scheduled. I was then referred to a different doctor who saw a cataract on my right eye. He did not take a history. He would later say that had he known I had a diagnosis of a detached retina under the cataract, he would not have operated. My aunt could have told him that. I could have told him that. A series of three or so operations were planned to remove the cataract by "stippling." All went well after the first operation. After the second, I had severe headaches. My aunt called him at least every other day except the weekend. His message was always the same: "Bring him back in two weeks."

In two weeks, my aunt took me to his office. Before I'd come even within ten feet of him, he told my aunt he would meet us at the hospital.

Glaucoma was setting in. They prescribed eye drops to counteract the glaucoma. Then that night they came to cut my eyelashes. I knew what that meant; they were planning to operate on me again—without telling me. I asked, "Does my mother know you are planning another operation?" When they refused to answer, I threw a verbal fit.

The next development I knew of was Mother and my siblings arriving in Boston. I saw them from the hospital window. Mother had bundled everyone up and taken a Pullman to come to Boston. I had a hard time imagining what that trip cost her emotionally. I was very appreciative. That was a major thaw in our cold war. I again felt loved and part of the family.

It was a Catholic hospital. There were crucifixes on the walls of every room. Feeling assertive and aggressive, I told my mother I wanted them taken down. "He has risen."

Mother said, "You are a guest in this hospital. The people who run the hospital put their emphasis on Jesus' death. We put it on His life and on the fact that He rose. This is a good hospital. They do a lot of good here. You will be respectful of their beliefs and will behave as a respectful guest."

I had the eye surgery.

The operation(s) were pronounced failures, and I was discharged with instructions to see the Navy doctors as soon as possible. We arrived in Norfolk, which happened to be on Halloween day.

Mother arranged an appointment for me with the Navy doctors within the week. After lengthy examinations, they said that my right eye had been so traumatized by operations and treatments with harsh eyedrops that my body was regarding it as foreign tissue and was reabsorbing it. The problem was that my body was reabsorbing both eyes. The eye would have to be removed, or I would become totally blind. They did remove it, and replaced it with a gold implant to keep an artificial eye from sinking deep into its socket.

My mother took me to Washington, D.C., to get my first glass eye. I had it before I started school the lower sixth grade in February. I had lost half a school year. That shift meant a new group of classmates, which in turn triggered a new round of fights to establish the pecking order. I didn't always win, but always gave a good accounting of myself, in part because I would take more pain than most fellows without quitting.

I realized I had a choice either to be ashamed of the eye or to make the best of it in the open. I chose the latter. By the third day of school, the girl seated behind me had become a pest, always borrowing something—a pencil, a sheet of paper. On the third or fourth day, instead of an eraser, I reached under my left arm with my glass eye on my right thumb. She let out a shriek. The teacher rushed to her. In the confusion, I slipped my glass eye back in its socket. The girl was partially incoherent, and had no credibility.

I would take my eye out and let other kids look for a nickel. It became so accepted that my classmates were betting other kids in school that I could take my eye out. Mother asked me where I came by so much money. She seemed satisfied by the explanation.

During spring cleaning that year, my mother turned my grandmother's mattress over. There she found an envelope with twenty-five crisp one-dollar bills in it. That should have exonerated me. It didn't. Mother accused me of replacing my grandmother's money with money I had gotten from showing off my glass eye.

I would have trouble judging distances, such as a baseball coming toward me, especially when trying to hit the ball. None of my peers wanted me on their side in baseball. I developed an inferiority complex in regard to sports. Then one day in physical education class, we played kickball with baseball rules using a soccer ball rolled over the plate. It was two-dimensional judging, not three-dimensional. I was surprisingly good at it. I understood the differences from baseball in my performance.

The cold war continued. Nevertheless, Mother saw to it that my religious education continued at home as well as at Sunday school. She read the *Bible* to me and assigned passages for me to read on my own. I was also to memorize certain passages.

In our home, misbehavior was usually dealt with by talking; more serious infractions resulted in spankings. Mother used a limber twig administered to the back of my bare legs. At the top of the list of serious infractions was lying. In that case, my siblings or I would get two punishments. One for the first infraction; the second and most severe was for lying. Lying was equated with bearing false witness.

Questioning Theology

By the age of eleven, I was questioning some of the discrepancies among the gospels. Mother explained that Matthew was a Jew and addressed his gospel to Jews. Mark was a Roman and addressed his gospel to Romans. Luke was Greek and addressed his gospel to them. John, a Jew, addressed his gospel to all humanity. This had an impact on the path I pursued. Paul Tillich expressed a similar idea when he said that the book of John is not so much a biography as the other gospels are; rather, it is a theological book. It is a reinterpretation of the life of Jesus in light of later theological problems.[3]

When I was twelve, Mother wanted me to be baptized and join the church. I told her I couldn't say I believed in Jesus as she held that I should. However, at her request, I agreed at least to talk with the minister. Mother would never suggest that I be anything but honest, nor would she have called the minister to brief him before the interview. She left it in the hands of God. There was a great deal of doubt in my mind about all this theology. It would be nice, if it were true. I foresaw the possibility—the distinct probability—of a time in the future that I would firmly disbelieve.

The preacher came to our house and asked me one question: "Do you take Jesus as your Lord and Savior?" This was not a question of belief. "To take" was a voluntary action—taking. I could "take" without misrepresenting myself—even to myself. Besides, there were no other options for "to take as Lord and Savior." My answer was late in coming, but I said, "Yes." I was baptized. It was some time before I realized it was merely different words for the same question. Today, I wonder if this experience was a root in my using the psychiatric distinctions among feeling, thinking, and acting as a tool to make comparisons among religions. I was unaware of any change in Mother's attitude toward me after I joined the church. She had met a parental responsibility.

Boy Scouts

On March 4, 1945, I joined the Boy Scouts at age twelve. It was a troop sponsored by our church, almost two miles away. I walked to the meetings. One evening I got a ride home with three or four high-school boys. In spite of my telling them, "My house is at the end of the block. Here it is!" they didn't slow up. They drove to an isolated spot at the end of the peninsula. They pulled me out of the car and held my wrists as I protested and struggled. There was a brief lull, during which I planned my moves. Maybe 100 yards to my right there was a boat dock closed off with a locked gate. I planned to knee the one who was holding me, a hard jab to the groin, then jerk free, run to the dock, and jump into the water. I would come up either under the dock or on the far side of a boat tied up there. I didn't think they would get wet. The dock was the opposite direction from the road and some houses. If I could knee him hard enough to put him on the ground, I would gain some time.

Before I could implement my plan, one of the men said, "This isn't right." Then to me, he said, "Get back in the car. We will take you home." I did and they did.

For the year in Norfolk, the Scouts had perhaps one or two campouts all year. In South Carolina with Scout-master John Meaney, we had a campout every month regardless of the weather, and on all types of terrain: sandy beach, woods, and mountains. I credit the scouting programs and its leaders both in Norfolk and Charleston for diverting me from delinquency.

Dad Returns

My father received thirty-day leave after the Battle of Okinawa. His ship, the *USS Custer*, APA 40, was an attack transport, as the one featured in the movie, *All Boats Away*, staring Jeff Chandler. The *USS Custer* had reduced the size of its ward room and made other changes to be able to carry two more landing craft. This enabled the ship to put its combat troops and their supplies ashore faster than others. They had also positioned the ship quite close to the beach. For the speed in unloading, the ship was cited and Captain Terry was awarded the Silver Star. Dad received a Commendation citation. After this landing was completed, Captain Terry asked permission to withdraw. That was denied; he was ordered to position his ship at the outside edge of the convoy and to pretend to be unloading. This made them prime targets for Japanese kamikaze attacks. The ship sustained two such attacks. In battle, Dad would order the fire hoses stretched out on decks with water pressure on, but shut off at the nozzle. If the ship was hit, the adjacent fire hose would break and immediately put water on the spot of the damage—apparently a standard practice. After Okinawa, the *Custer* limped into Portland, Oregon. Dad had been in three naval-battle landings: Layette, Luzon, and Okinawa. He had also made several non-battle landings.

We picked Dad up at the airport at about 11:30 a.m. one August day in 1945, a happy occasion. At about 2 p.m., I noticed Dad sitting in a car talking with my aunt. "How did she get there?" I wondered. As I approached the car, Dad told me to leave them alone. I did. One or two hours later, Dad came to me and said, "You have to promise me that you will obey your mother, or I'll take you anywhere in town you want to go and drop you off. You will be on your own. You have till sundown to let me know." He had not asked me anything about my side of it. I had been "put on report" by my aunt, and Dad acted. I had not disobeyed Mother. I had given her a hard time, but for Dad that would be a technicality. I counted my money: $22.55. Only twelve years old, I considered being a Huck Finn on the river, going into Norfolk and shining shoes for servicemen, but I was aware of harassment, including sexual harassment. I considered going to a relative's house, but they would call my parents right away and be told that I stole money. That would preclude my best option with an adult cousin who ran a store. I didn't think my allergies and asthma to dust and pollen would allow me to work on a farm.

About a half-hour before sundown, I capitulated. I had no doubt that Dad would follow through. I became depressed. Dad was clearly willing to get rid of me. I empathized with Isaac, whose father, Abraham, was also willing to get rid of him. Abraham didn't even argue or plead with God for his son's life, yet he had pleaded with Him to save the city of Sodom. If fifty righteous men were found in the city, then the number was reduced to ten. Genesis 18:23-33

Mother might or might not protest, but Dad would do it. The relative I was closest to was my aunt, who had been talking to Dad. She had flown from Boston to Norfolk just to talk with Dad about me. Was there an option I was overlooking? For the next couple of years these questions occupied my mind while other fellows were thinking of women and being sports heroes.

It was a year or two before I identified a reasonable alternative path: I might have left, taking my $22.55 along with some food, clothes, and scouting gear—my knife, compass, blankets, matches, flashlight, and scout handbook with my name torn off because I couldn't take anything with my name on it. I would spend the night across the road, sleeping on the ground. There was a bus stop nearby. I could walk to a bus stop farther away— "downstream"—to catch an early bus in the morning. I would ride into Norfolk and to the ferry terminal that went to Newport

News, Virginia. The river and ferry formed a psychological barrier.

In Newport News, I would seek out a large Baptist church, go inside, and ask for sanctuary. I could and would tell them everything except my true name. I might use Mark Spivens or Mark Phelps as an alias, names I would automatically be alert to. I would say that Dad had returned from the war a different man. He wanted time alone with Mother, and I was in the way, so he threw me out. I also needed to be careful not to give them identifying information on Dad—or on Mom, for that matter. To questions about my family, I would simply remain silent. I knew that if I talked at all on those topics, they might well figure me out.

I wasn't concerned about Dad coming after me. He wouldn't. I was concerned about the authorities making Dad take me back. That would have been hell!

I figured my ticket to sanctuary was my knowledge of the *Bible*, which I could put on display, even reciting whole chapters. I would stress the scripture on separating the sheep from the goats in Matthew 25:31-46. "Those things you have done for others, you have done for me: I was hungry and you fed me, I was homeless and you took me in."

In my mind I did compose a letter to Dad: "I am sorry you lost two sons. This son, you just threw away. I did not steal my grandmother's money." However, by the time I thought of all this, the time had passed.

Dad didn't stay home the full month. After about a week or ten days, he received orders to go to Connecticut for training, then to Charleston, South Carolina, to serve as executive officer on the *USS Tidewater*, AD31, a destroyer tender.

Somehow Dad got permission for me to live on the ship for a week or two. I was not consulted. That was a miserable time. Dad said he assumed one of the men would take me under his wing, but that didn't happen. I'm sure I sent many nonverbal messages to leave me alone.

Nothing had changed at home while I was aboard the ship. I was not cheered up; I did not feel closer to anyone. Maybe Mother got something out of it. I hope so. My fights on the playground intensified. Two of my scouting friends were arrested for stealing street signs. I had declined to join them and told them, "That is dangerous; someone could get hurt or even killed."

In June 1946 when I was thirteen, my family followed Dad to Charleston, South Carolina. We moved into a rented house across the street from my aunt and uncle, who had been transferred from Boston to Charleston earlier. On the first or second day, I was walking around, casing the neighborhood, when I came upon a vacant-lot football game with maybe a dozen players. I asked if I could play. "Yes," came the reply. "Get in the line right there." I was on defense. When the ball was snapped, I tore into the opponent's backfield and threw them for a loss. I was slow getting up—grandstanding; I wanted everyone to see the tackle I had made. Then I heard a voice, "You can get up now." It was a feminine voice. I looked at the person's face. Yes, the legs I was holding belonged to a good-looking girl. We became sweethearts.

My father's sister, an inner-city high-school teacher in Louisville, Kentucky, came to Charleston to spend a month to six weeks with us. She helped me with reading, and we did a lot of sightseeing around Charleston. Under her prodding, I made a scrapbook of some of the places we visited.

On our porch sat a wooden box six feet long. It was full of old comic books left by a previous tenant. I had not been allowed to have any comics except Walt Disney and Donald Duck. Lacking confidence in my reading skills, I simply looked through them.

Then when I got bored, I tried reading them. I surprised myself by actually being able to read them.

Trip to Kentucky

After thirty-three months' separation, my parents needed some time alone. Dad arranged for Sallie and me to visit Dad's brothers in Wayne County, Kentucky. We traveled by ourselves on the train. We got off the train in Burnside. It was about 2:30 a.m. Uncle Dave wasn't there. I took Sallie up two long flights of steps up a steep hill to an all-night tavern. The lady there was quite kind. I delayed accepting her invitation to put Sallie to bed for about an hour. I had just given in to it when Uncle Dave walked in. Both Uncle Dave and Uncle Al were farmers, and my grandfather currently lived in the area. While there we saw wheat harvested via a combine, and watched a contractor install indoor plumbing, replacing the well and long dipper pail.

When I was thirteen, sometime during the late summer of 1946, my cousin, Mother's sister's son, came running across the street to our house: "Marshall, Marshall, you didn't steal Grandmother's money."

"I have known that from the beginning, but how do you know it?"

"Because she just accused me of the same thing."

I was vindicated, accepted by Mother and the whole clan.

Years later, after Dad's death in 1964, I told Dad's brother, Uncle Bob, about all of this. At the end, I added, "I don't know if he really would have followed through."

With conviction my uncle said, "Of course he would have."

I asked, "What makes you so sure?"

He said, "Two things. He would have known that if he didn't, he would lose all control over you." That was one I had realized.

I asked, "What's the other reason?"

My uncle said, "Because *his* father did that to *him*."

When Dad was ten or eleven, and his mother called him to supper, Dad had gotten on his bike and ridden away. That is where the "If you don't promise to obey your mother…" had come from, even though it didn't fit my situation.

I had completed the lower half of seventh grade in Norfolk. South Carolina didn't have mid-year promotions. For me, it was either repeat the first half of the seventh or skip the second half. They were in different buildings with different principals. Mother took me to the principal of the eighth-grade school. I was placed in the eighth grade "on condition."

That year I made one A and one C, and the rest were B's.

Quasi-delinquency

I was on the muscle, feeling assertive and aggressive. For many years, I have considered this period in my life as the quasi-delinquent period. On the first or second day of school, I bet J.C. Keagen fifty cents that I could break any hold he got on me. I allowed him to get his hold. He got a head lock on me. When he said he was ready, I put my knee under his buttocks and threw myself and him backward. His head hit the handle of a locker, cutting his scalp. Head wounds usually bleed profusely; his wound was no exception. I don't recall that I ever collected that fifty cents. Most of my delinquencies were trespasses. My friends and I were shot at; at least, we heard the bullets whiz through the air.

One day my buddy took a pistol to school. When transferring it from one pocket to another, it went off. The bullet tore off the tip of one of his fingers and lodged in a teacher's desk.

My friend's finger bled profusely. There was a trail of blood to the boy's lavatory. He asked to borrow my handkerchief to wrap around his finger to help stop the bleeding. As luck would have it, the handkerchief I had that day was the one on which my sweetheart had embroidered my initials. When my friend got the bleeding stopped, he threw the handkerchief away in the trash can in the boy's lavatory. The police found it there. The talk around school was someone had attempted to murder the teacher. My initials were easily identified as mine. I was called to the principal's office to talk with the police shortly before the end of school.

Near the end of the school year, they announced that all of us were to have IQ tests. I had a discussion with myself:

> Why are they giving us IQ tests?
> To determine how smart we are.
> Why?
> To measure our potential.
> Why?
> Because they are going to grade us on a curve with our potential being a consideration—at least they are thinking about it. Therefore, the thing to do is not score too high on the IQ test.

Come test time, I took the first two-thirds seriously and marked the remainder at random. My official IQ, the only one I ever took, showed a score of 89. I started getting A's. I was pretty proud of myself. However, the better grades were probably due to my brain maturation at puberty. I saw no evidence of adjusted grades secondary to assumed potential.

Grandmother's Return

Dad had minimal time away from his ship. Mother worked as a school teacher. Sometime in 1947, the year I turned fourteen, my aunt and her family moved to the Washington, D.C., area, and my grandmother moved back in with us.

Football in Gym Class

Near the beginning of school my ninth-grade year, my gym teacher, who was also the football coach, had the class scrimmaging against each other. I was placed in a tackle position, opposing Cliff Tucker, a fellow half a head taller, one to two years older, and heavier—more muscular. I never got into his backfield; he got into mine only once all afternoon. I was satisfied with myself. As we left the field, I was surprised to see Dad. He had been watching me all afternoon. That evening he complimented me on my play. I learned much later that he had contacted the coach and asked him not to recruit me for fear that playing might cause a detached retina in my good eye. I appreciated that. I had some idea of what my playing would mean to him. He had made his desires subordinate to my welfare. I felt loved and protected.

The Wrong Kind of Church

My parents had been sending me to a neighborhood Baptist church four blocks from our house. They didn't attend because my senile grandmother needed constant supervision, and my father's duties with the Navy usually kept him away. At the new church, I realized how hypocritical our preacher was. My parents didn't believe what I was telling them. After a year or so, my grandmother again moved in with my aunt, my father was out of the Navy, and my parents started going to church. After attending a few services, they moved their membership some twenty miles away to Citadel Square Baptist Church in Charleston. Each parent made repeated statements for me to disregard that experience. "It was not representative of Christianity."

The Bus-stop Building

In the spring of 1947, my parents bought a 15-acre tract on which to build the new house. Six acres were solid ground. Nine acres were tidal marsh. There were majestic trees. The land was overgrown with all sorts of vegetation. A spur railroad line formed one boundary. The railroad crossed the marsh on wooden trestles and went to oil terminals along the Cooper River, then to the paper mill, which processed 139 railroad cars of pulp wood a day. The railroad and the river had been determining factors in selecting the site for a port of embarkation. By 1947, the site had been declared war surplus. It was divided into tracts and sold at public auction. Those who purchased the assets had to clear the land in a specified time. They did so by selling the property in smaller lots. Dad bought a portion of a building in this manner. He hired a house mover to move his purchase some twelve miles or so to the new lot for the family to live in while the new house was being built.

There was a 10 by 30' roofed bus stop; it was enclosed on three sides. I went to the office to find out who owned it. The real-estate plats were not clear about that, but it had to be one of two people. I went to one and asked to buy the bus-stop building. He said he didn't own it. I asked, if you do, may I have it? He said, "Yes." Then I went to the other possible owner. We had a similar conversation. I arranged with the house mover to also move my bus-stop building for $35. When I told Dad about it, he asked where I was going to put it. I told him, on the back of the property near the marsh. Dad said, "You can't put your building on my land. Besides, I need it to put an office in to track building supplies and workmen's time. I'll pay you what you have in it." He placed the bus-stop building next to the driveway at the front of the lot.

Work on building the new home didn't get started that summer. Dad hadn't finished the plans. I am unaware of any financial arrangements, except for money from the sale of the Norfolk house. Dad bought an investment property in the summer or fall. Two apartments were renovated, and a four-lot house-trailer park was built. Mother must have foreseen the future events, for she took a job teaching third grade in September.

Summer Scouting

In the summer of 1947, I was a member of the Scout summer-camp staff. I was responsible for the camp store. Among other things, I sold the supplies for the handicraft programs. Somehow, "Rocky," the scout in charge of the handicraft program, and I became miffed at each other. The miff extended through the last part of the summer. When camp was over, part of our compensation was a week of camping and canoeing on Fontana Lake behind a man-made dam in North Carolina. Our camp director was very obese. He had two canoes lashed together. He occupied one seat, and he assigned his "waterfront" crew to the other three seats. After 25 paddle strokes, one of the four would rest. This meant that there were only three paddling at any one time.

As I looked at the parings for the other canoes, I noticed that Rocky and I were assigned to different canoes, he with a scout who was a goof-off and I to a three-man canoe. I went to Rocky, showed him the posted pairings, and suggested we request to be assigned to the same canoe. Rocky saw the wisdom in that. Together we went to the director with our request. He agreed. With the three best waterfront guys tied up with the two canoes lashed together, Rocky and I got the role of exploring different inlets. This included finding campsites for the night. Rocky and I got along well. The camp director took credit for healing the rift.

In the Scouts I earned the rank of Eagle. I was the youngest teenager in that Coastal Carolina Scout Council to earn it. I was elected by my peers to the Order of the Arrow and later was awarded the status of "Brother." I was vice-chair of our lodge, 236. I was senior Scout of a jamboree, which planted over five-thousand pine-tree seedlings. Dad served on the Scout committee and presided at some Courts of Honor. I appreciated his support.

Dad's Discharge

In the fall of 1947, Dad was admitted to the naval hospital due to complications from his service-related disability, a peptic ulcer. He had surgery for the bleeding ulcer. By this time, many servicemen were being discharged. Dad wanted Navy retirement, which would include commissary privileges. To qualify, a person had to be on continuous active duty for eight years. His eight years would be completed on January 1, 1948. He tried to transfer from the reserves to regular Navy, but was told he was too old and, as Commander, had too much rank. He was discharged December 25, 1947, during his surgical recuperation. He had an outstanding service record, but being in the hospital could have been interpreted as "gold-bricking," and maybe that contributed to his sudden discharge.

He could have been voluntarily separated from the service anytime in 1946 or 1947. Had he done so, his reception by college personnel officials might well have been much more favorable. In fact, two colleges told him they had enough trouble with veterans who were students; they certainly didn't need one on the faculty.

These rejections and disappointments undoubtedly had a significant effect on his self-esteem as well as financially. As a result, his frustration tolerance became problematic. Prior to the war, I don't remember him getting angry over next to nothing (e.g.: a jacket that falls from its hook as it is being hung up). These explosions were only verbal and not aimed at anyone in particular.

Mother and Dad had a very loving relationship; however, Mother would not stand up to Dad either for herself or for the family. I did not want a wife similar to my mother in this regard. I wanted a wife who would tell me directly what she thought. I wanted a wife whose opinion would be valuable, sometimes better than mine.

Dad asked his sister Nanny Taylor, who owned a successful Western Auto store with her husband, Ray Taylor, whether to put the money from the Norfolk house into the new home or into a business. She replied, "The business can support the house; the house cannot support the business."

Dad's dream was to build a home he could be proud of. Temporarily he (they) gave up their rental house for the mess-hall kitchen from the port of embarkation's surplus war asset. The family moved in before the fourth wall was closed in, perhaps a year or two later. Two rooms were added, and it was sided. They didn't entertain in that house, as they had entertained in the Norfolk house. Mom and Dad entertained some in the Officer's Club and in the yard.

Dad needed to achieve three goals: generate an income, build a home for the family, and secure an adequate retirement. He took a position as a ninth-grade science teacher. Unfortunately, he did not prioritize his goals, nor did he keep centered on any one goal. Mother continued to teach third grade.

Dad tried to start a concrete-slag block business incorporating slag from the steel mill. The product was a good one, but was never promoted. In this endeavor he hired two African-American men: Isaac Campbell and Isaac Gathers. Isaac Campbell remained a friend in our lives. Dad was instrumental in helping him obtain a job as custodian of North Charleston Elementary School.

It was during this period that Dad got angry at me about something that I didn't think I deserved. In the middle of his chewing me out, I began to chew him out for the first time in my life. He became very quiet. When I ran out of things to say, he said, "You have the right to get angry at me, and I have the right to get angry at you. As long as we don't get angry at each other at the same time, we will be okay. *But this was my time!*" With that he walked away.

Self-esteem

Early adolescent self-esteem is determined by the answers one gives himself or herself to two questions: "How lovable am I?" and "How adequate am I?" As adolescents grow into adulthood, they also begin answering "How respected am I?" either as a separate question or as part of the adequacy question. Most young people get their answers to the lovable question from parents and, later, from a sweetheart. Teachers and other role models will influence this answer somewhat, as will approval from peers. Some adolescent sexual exploration is a search for this re-assurance.

I had felt loved by my mother and grandmother until they accused me of stealing, which is when the "cold war" developed. Not having another source, I tried to meet all my self-esteem needs by overcompensating with a strong sense of adequacy. Hence, I engaged in numerous playground fights where the power of one's adversary is often taken as a good indication of one's adequacy. And what better opponent than the police? My buddy and I once even challenged the police to "come and get us" from a 12-inch beam thirty feet above the ground.

I had hoped that joining the church as imother wished would result in less hostility from her—a net increase in love. That did not happen, so those dynamics began to fade as they were replaced by achievements in the Scouts. I earned approval from the leaders by advancing, which strengthened my sense of adequacy, control, and power. I do credit the Scouts for me not becoming an outright delinquent.

I continued to build on my sense of achievement through plumbing, then by working at the locker club where I was holding my own with sailors several years older than I.

The Locker Club

Dad was also looking at a number of other business opportunities. The U.S. economy took a downturn in February 1948, which triggered the sale of a large building just outside the main gate of the Navy Yard. Dad purchased the property. He planned to operate a locker club for sailors there. It would give sailors a place to store civilian clothes, change into them, go out on the town, then change back into uniform before returning to their ships. It would be a pleasant, hassle-free place from which to start a liberty. In full operation, in addition to renting lockers, we would sell some clothes, operate a snack bar, and offer nine beds so a few men could sleep there. The building needed a lot of renovation: new wiring, new plumbing, and showers. We had to procure and install the lockers. Dad did all the plumbing, and I was his helper. I was also the electrician's helper. Because Dad bought the building on a GI home loan, we would have to live in it for six months. Both Mother and Dad continued to teach school.

We opened for business in September 1949. It would always have to be open. The carpenter took the 7 a.m. shift. I worked from 3 to 11 p.m., and Dad from 11 p.m. to 7 a.m. After 7 p.m. or so, there was very little traffic, so that was my study time. The locker-club responsibility ended my pre-delinquency, as well as my scouting career. The family needed me, so I was there, even if I wasn't loved. The sailors got paid every two weeks in the afternoon. Dad set me up to collect locker rent and payments on their charge accounts. I also did the books for the club. Shortly, the locker club had a waiting list for lockers. I urged Dad to increase the monthly locker fee. He wouldn't. He was part social worker. I would have continued with scouting had it not been for "the locker club."

One day in the locker club, a sailor tried to sell me a pea-coat, a warm winter coat. This one had another sailor's name stenciled in it, which had not been canceled by a red "DC" through the name. Further, I knew the second sailor. Later, I asked him about it.

Ultimately, Naval Intelligence got involved. There had been a number of thefts aboard that ship. Now they had the culprit. He received a bad-conduct discharge, and may have served time in the brig. He paid his bill and emptied his locker. Then he asked for his gun we had in safekeeping, a .38 Special. I got the gun and gave it to him. As I did so, he said, "I ought to give you this right in the gut." I believed the most dangerous thing I could do was show fear. I said, "Here is your ammunition." He took the gun and ammo, then left. I wasn't all that concerned, but I called Dad and told him. He said to get out of there. "Don't try to secure anything; just get out. I'm on my way." I left the building and concealed myself in the shrubbery. Nothing more occurred on this issue.

I worked those shifts during my junior and senior years of high school. Every third week, one of us had a day off; and every third week, one of us pulled a sixteen-hour shift. When we opened the snack bar, Dad also hired some of his students to staff it.

When I started college, my classes were only twenty miles from the club, so I commuted and slept at the club most nights. I had biology lab Monday afternoons, but other than that, I worked at the club as before. The locker-club work precluded most social life. I had one date in all my freshman year. I realized my experience with women was deficient; I joined a social fraternity, Pi Kappa Phi, and later became president of the Alpha Chapter in my junior year. I did not resent any of this. Many of the antics my classmates described seemed inane or even stupid; they were the ones acting macho. I was doing better than holding my own with sailors.

Decision To Go to Medical School

When I decided to go to medical school, I had more courses with labs to meet the entrance requirements, so I moved into the college gymnasium. I was the only person there at night. I was home on weekends, and still did the books. At the start of the second semester, Jessie Sparks, a fraternity brother, invited me to move in with him in the Episcopal Diocesan headquarters, rent-free, and help him as janitor for the building. One Sunday, Jessie called to say that the rector had consecrated too much wine for communion. It had to be consumed, not poured or allowed to sit around in bottles. I made sure the rector knew I considered myself an atheist, but I would be glad to lend my throat and stomach to the Church in such an emergency. The three of us lounged in the churchyard that beautiful Sunday afternoon, relieving the Holy Ghost from the confines of his wine bottles.

God's Involvement

I had viewed my brother's death as a natural phenomenon devoid of any supernatural elements. He had rolled over and over until he got a spindle of the bedstead across his windpipe and suffocated. To declare it an act of God was to come face to face with "the problem of evil"; namely, How could an all-loving, omniscient, omnipotent, and intervening God allow evil in the world, both natural evil (storms, earthquakes, etc.) and human evil? The answers I gave myself were on three levels:

1. If heaven was as it had been pictured, then God would love us whether we were on earth or in heaven, and presumably it would make little or no difference to God where we were. Therefore, the question itself was false. On the other hand, one of the functions of all religions is to help the living cope with crises of this world.

2. If God did not intervene in human affairs, humans must have complete free choice in their actions. This is the same conclusion Rabbi Harold Kushner published years later in *Why Bad Things Happen to Good People.*[4]

3. God was not involved.

News of the Holocaust only strengthened these conclusions.
Later, I was further put off by the biblical book of Job. I had known most of the story of Job, of how the devil challenged God, asserting that Job would turn against God if severe calamities befell Job. To test Job, God gave the devil control over everything except Job's life. God allowed the devil to take all of Job's wealth (his livestock) and caused all of his children to die. The book concludes by saying that Job was righteous in God's eyes, and God bestowed more wealth and more children on Job than he had before. The moral of the story was Job's steadfastness in his love of God.

Perhaps this was a rich and fitting reward for Job, but what about those who were killed? Didn't they count? Even as an allegory, this story was (is) flawed. These were not the actions of a just God, but a story from an extremely patriarchal society.

I knew the concepts of heaven and hell after death were based on belief in Jesus, and on earned rewards or punishments for one's acts of goodness and badness during life. I interpreted these concepts as an adult version of the Santa Clause story, with switches and ashes for children who had been bad, and presents for those who had been good. (See Exhibit B.)

I believed in human kinship with animals. Dogs were loyal and loving. If humans had a heaven, then why not animals? Later, after studying Hinduism and Jainism, I noted the similarities of the myths. The Indians must have faced the same questions I had, and they answered them with the doctrines of karma and reincarnation. These doctrines also were used to justify the caste system of Indian Hinduism. "You be a good and respectful member of your lower caste, thereby storing up your karma, and in the next round of rebirth, you may well be born into a higher caste." Jainism extended these concepts to all animals.

My doubts and questioning continued. I struggled with those two questions of how people were to be saved when they never had the opportunity to believe in Jesus—those born before Jesus' time and those who never even had the opportunity to hear of him. God has always been represented as fair and just. I realized there were only two possible answers: either God would have to send a messenger to every culture, or the key to the good life and salvation was innate and at least partially discoverable by anyone who was seeking—or both answers were correct.

I Am An Atheist

In my mid-teens, I hesitated to take "the final step" of declaring myself a non-believer—even to myself. I framed the question to myself as, "Do I have a right to question all of this Christianity?" despite the fact that I had been questioning it for years. I spent hours on end in solitude, walking the railroad tracks that cut through the woods beside our house, contemplating that question. After a year and a half to two years, I concluded that if God gave me and all humans the ability to contemplate and to reason, he intended us to use it. God could have made humans like that insect, the praying mantis, always assuming the praying position when at rest. But then what of free will? I concluded that I did have the right to question. With this conclusion and the awareness that I did not believe in any deity, I openly considered myself an atheist.

During a year or so of my strong atheist days, my brother was leading his high school in school prayer over the PA system. I was an evangelistic atheist; but when I realized I was hurting others, I became a more respecting and compassionate atheist.

I was aware of some similarity of the characteristics attributed to God and to Santa. However, except for my intellectual awareness of the similarity, they remained distinct. Both personalities are depicted as omniscient. "You better be good, I'm telling you why: Santa Clause is coming to town… He knows if you've been bad or good, so be good for goodness' sake." The levels of "knowing" were of entirely different order of magnitude. God was global, all-encompassing; Santa's range only included Christmas and earning the reward of toys. God was more powerful than Santa, even though Santa had magic (e.g., flying reindeer). God had everything; He only had to think a thought. One could talk to God through prayer, but one had to write to Santa. (Mother or Dad would hear my prayers every night; Mother would have a hand on me during this time.) The other thing that helped me maintain the separateness was the tone and attitude of reverence while talking with God versus the boisterousness of the Christmas music I associated with Santa.

Since those high-school years, I have not been an anti-religious person. I do not search for ways to put down religion. When I find incidents of religious inconsistency, I feel sad, as if one of my friends has stumbled. I do lay out many of the issues, such as the two that plagued me after my brother's death.

Between High School and College

After high-school graduation, I was offered a good job by the head of a plumbing firm who was familiar with my skills, but I turned it down to go to college. I enjoyed learning for its own sake, but perhaps equally importantly, I saw college as a way out of my father's business without receiving a heavy guilt trip.

Throughout the years of the Korean conflict, I was classified 4F by my draft board because of my glass eye.

The rest of my family attended Citadel Square Baptist Church. Reverend Wallace Rogers was pastor. I went several times, enough to determine that their message was not for me. I was content with my formulations of "love is God" and considered myself an atheist.

Several days before college started for me as a nineteen-year-old in my sophomore year, September 1952, my grandmother who had been living with us died. There was a religious service locally. She was to be buried in her husband's cemetery plot in Lincolnton, North Carolina, a 238-mile trip one way. Dad expressed some doubts as to whether our family's twelve-year-old car could make the trip. Dad said this in an offhanded way, whereupon Reverend Wallace Rogers offered to lend his car to Dad and the family, which Dad accepted. I was struck by the generosity of that offer. Reverend Rogers truly lived what he preached. The rest of my family continued at Citadel Square Church for several years.

I Choose a Medical School

During the summer of 1952, I decided I wanted to go to the Medical College of South Carolina. Finances made the decision of where to enroll easy; my family could only possibly afford the state-supported school. My parents supported the decision. Although I would need to take a heavy science load to meet the entrance requirement and compensate for not taking chemistry my freshman year, I applied after only three years of college, a practice that was passé. I didn't expect to be admitted that year, but I hoped to learn the ropes. My personal interview was with the professor of physiology:

Dr. Kinand: "I see you are applying after only three years of college."

I: "Yes, sir. What does that do for me?"

Dr. Kinand: "It puts you in a less-preferred category. And I see you have not had either French or German, only Spanish."

I: "Yes, sir. I understand the college has accepted Spanish for the language requirement."

Dr. Kinand: "We have, rarely."

I: "What is the impact on me?"

Dr. Kinand: "It puts you in a less-preferred category. I see your grades are not all that good. How do you account for that?"

I: "Yes, sir. I am a poor speller, and my professors rightly take off for it. What is the impact on me?"

Dr. Kinand: "It puts you in a less-preferred category."

I received notice that they had filled the class without me.

That summer, I enrolled in George Washington University in Washington, D.C. I lived with my aunt and uncle and rode with my uncle as he went to work at the Navy Department. I would study in the library, then meet my uncle for the ride back to his house. I took six hours of French and three hours of psychology—nine semester hours in eight weeks. I made an 89 in one course and a 90 in the other. I had a transcript sent to the med school. I spent time with my cousin, four years younger, and helped my uncle with some projects. I planned to take a second year of French and pull up my grades. That would eliminate all three "less-preferred categories." College started mid-September.

Back at the locker club on a hot Wednesday after Labor Day, I was drilling holes in wood over my head with sawdust and wood shavings in my hair and down my bare back, when Mother called. "A Miss Harper called, saying that if you want to go to medical school this fall, you are to be at her office at 7:45 in the morning." I was there. One of the students they had accepted was later accepted at Duke University Medical School and had gone there. The legislature required the school to start with a class of 80, so I was a replacement. Later I learned the admission committee was monitoring my progress closely. I placed in the middle third of the class, which was all the information they provided.

Racial Issue

My social fraternity had been founded at our institution, the College of Charleston, in 1904. The 50th anniversary of the fraternity convention was to be in Charleston in 1954. I had been Archon (president) the last semester of the '53 school year. The '54 convention was to vote on removing all references and limitations against blacks at the convention. Jessie Sparks, as current president, cast the first vote for the eliminations of discrimination. The next fourteen chapters followed our lead in voting to eliminate racial prohibitions. Most of these colleges were in the South; one was in California. The vote to eliminate all racial references carried by a wide margin. I had done considerable campaigning for that vote.

I Fall In Love—A Catholic Woman

I was a happy atheist. Nothing of significance happened in my spiritual or religious life until the spring I turned 22 in 1955. I was finishing my first year of medical school. A mile or so away at my college my former classmates were celebrating spring with dances. I attended two or three of them. At one, I met a Catholic woman with whom I fell in love over the summer.

During the '55-56 school year, our relationship deepened. We went to a Catholic league basketball game. One of the teams was her former high-school team. I noticed a group of nuns and a priest on the sidelines. I asked my date what they were doing. She said they were saying the rosary and praying for their team. On the opposite side of the court there was a similar group of nuns and a priest. They, too, were praying for victory. I asked my date how God was going to decide between them. She replied, "By whichever group led the most virtuous lives." I had thought such ideas had gone out in the Middle Ages with the concept of trial by mortal combat.

One Sunday I went with her to mass; my lack of familiarity with the service was quite obvious to all. The women of her church rallied around her.

Psychologically, I was committed to her. We each had two more years of schooling, and there were issues of financial support, but I did not see any other problems for the relationship. Her father was Lutheran, a fact that probably caused people around her to be more dedicated to seeing her remain Catholic. My sense of the rest of her family's attitude toward her father was, "He is a nice guy, but he is just not in the know, something of a second-class family member." When I contemplated my religion, I could not see any problems. Love was all encompassing. When I contemplated hers, the road seemed somewhat rocky, but still looked clear.

In the late spring, I invited her to a dinner dance of my fraternity. It was on a Friday night. The organizers asked for a count of those who wanted beef versus fish. I passed this option on to her. She chose beef. I expressed some surprise. She said something to the effect of "no big deal." However, at the dinner, she said she could not eat meat. I arranged to get her a fish meal. On talking about it later, she acknowledged her earlier statements, but explained her change of mind. "If someone who knew I was Catholic saw me eating meat, it might weaken their faith." My heart sank. This was a dimension I had not considered. It was one thing to respect and live with her choices and convictions. It was another to be faced with the Catholic community! Shortly she married a man who converted to Catholicism for her.

The Religious Study Group

In 1955, I discovered and read *The Spiritual Development of St. Paul* by George Matheson.[6] The book led me to further consider my own spiritual path. In the winter of that year, *Life* magazine published a series of articles on the great religions of the world. That summer, I planned to go to Mexico "on the cheap" with Jack Wilson, a friend and fraternity brother, just to bum around. My father wanted me to stay in the area and help him build the new home. It was to be started in two weeks. All summer long it was to start "in two weeks." This resulted in time on my hands. As it happened, there were four of my friends who also had time on their hands that summer. We were all going to graduate school in the fall. Paul Weidner organized a study group around the great religions using the *Life* magazine series as a starting point. I went along for the camaraderie. Paul was going to NYC to study stage production. Herman Williams, who had been a high-school classmate of mine, was going to enter a Baptist seminary in the fall. Jessie Sparks was set to enter an Episcopalian seminary. Jack

Wilson was scheduled to return to the University of North Carolina as a second-year graduate student in English. (Later I stood as his best man.) I was to enter my second year of medical school.

Paul assigned himself Hinduism. As I was seated next to Paul, he assigned me Buddhism. We met weekly throughout the summer.

That study group was a turning point for me. I was struck by several facts:

First: Some religions were clearly discovered; Buddhism had a founder. The four noble truths and the eight-fold path were straightforward. The way to live was prescribed without reference to a supernatural being or to an ungroundable faith, except for the doctrines of karma and reincarnation. There was no supernaturalism in Confucianism either.

Second: In spite of the differences in doctrines and supernatural beliefs, there are remarkable similarity among the religions. This is especially true in the areas of feeling and prescribed behavior. They all prescribe some form of The Golden Rule. They all prescribe giving alms and forgiving transgressions by fellow members of their religion, if not all humankind. They all preach social justice and advocate compassion, empathy, and love for fellow religious followers, if not all humanity.

Third: Many of the religious precepts were discovered in a mystic state. Mystics generally realized they had found a Truth. They also recognized that their understanding was (is) partial or incomplete. As a result they were generally humble. They often used local cultural metaphors to explain their insights, which might not be meaningful in a different locality or at a different time. They were also aware of gaps in their understanding; their well-meaning followers recognized and grasped many universal truths from the mystic. In time, these gaps in understanding tend to be filled in with that which seems right. In time, the distinction between what was original and what was filled in becomes obscure.

Fourth: Religions do change. In many instances, within a few hundred years of the original teaching, the religion undergoes significant transformation, often becoming more rigid, self-protective, and self-serving. Judaism has moved away from strict Orthodoxy, allowing individuals and congregations to conduct services in common languages. Many Protestant denominations now allow women to be ordained; some recognize homosexual relationships and even marriages. The Roman Catholic Church held Vatican II, which allowed services to be conducted in secular language and for the priest to face the congregation. Buddhists are moving from a strictly monastery place for worship to more secular settings. Many of the changes are attributed to God. For example, for many years a man could secure an animal to make a burnt sacrificial offering of it. God did not want these people gouged by insistence on a change of money to buy an animal. Jesus called the money changers robbers, and he drove them from the Temple. (Matthew 21:15-18) God banned burnt offerings, calling them a stench to his nostrils, instead advocating that people provide for the widows and orphans. Changes to religions have been occurring throughout history.

Fifth: There is something intrinsic within humans that seeks something "greater than the self." My readings of shamanism reinforced this conclusion. A portion of this desire is motivated by the felt need for supernatural help for some of life's difficulties. Several reasons stand out as to why the supernatural might wish to aid humans.

Supernatural Agents Have Interest In Humans

1. If the supernatural agents were spirits of ancestors, then it would be quite natural that the spirits had a vested interest in the well-being of their descendants and their society.

2. A covenant existed between the supernatural and the society—later the individual. The 10 Commandments are part of that covenant. "I shall be your God and you shall be my people."[5]

3. Perhaps God needed or craved to be worshiped.

4. Some form of bribery or payment was made to the supernatural, such as payment to the officials of the temple of Delos, or a special sacrifice to honor the supernatural.

5. Often rites and rituals accompanied requests. Sometimes the rituals were thought to be so powerful as to compel the supernatural to comply. The most common explanation given for the supernatural not acting favorably was that the rituals were not performed properly. This concept gave rise to ritual specialists. The Hindus believed that the rituals had to be sung in the proper pitch and that a ritual performed improperly could cause trouble.[7]

Perhaps most importantly, I saw that *all religions, including Christianity, espouse the love of fellow humans.* Some religions draw a small circle that may include only their village, their tribe, or their ethnicity, but a few do extend their circle to all humans. Some religions make an exception for those who attack their religion.

I also noticed a remarkable parallel between the teachings of Buddha and those of Jesus. I saw that both of these religions had developed out of an older tradition.

Further, I came to believe that *Jesus is (was) the personification of love.* This simple fact was sufficient for me to consider him the Son of Love—God. At the time of Jesus, the Greek influence was high. Greek gods were believed to have had sexual intercourse with mortals, and several gods were born from such unions. The story of Jesus' birth fit this pattern, too.

The gospels of Matthew, Mark, and Luke describe the earthly life of Jesus the man; whereas, the writings of John describe the role he fulfilled. The gospel of John begins with the Logos. John was writing for all humankind.

I took seriously and literally John's statements that God is spirit and those who worship him must do so in spirit and truth. Further, I inverted one of John's other sentences, from "God is love" to "Love is God." I was well aware that by the rules of grammar as well as those of logic, I was not justified in making this inversion.

My Name Substitution Trial

To test this formulation, I reread St. John, John 1, John 2, and John 3 in the *Bible*, substituting "the Totality of Love" for all references to God, substituting "the Personification of Love" for all references to Jesus, and substituting "the Spirit of Love" for any reference to the Holy Spirit. This test of John's writing stood up to these substitutions, and in some instances, they were more intelligible—at least to me. This reinforced my concept that love of fellow humans is the path to the good life—the best way to live, even without the concepts of salvation. This path is innate and discoverable by many different individuals in various different circumstances, with or without knowledge of Jesus. For example:

John 3:16: "For God so loved the world that he gave his only begotten son, that whosoever believed in him would not perish, but have everlasting life."

With substitution it becomes: *For the Totality of Love so loved the world that he gave his only begotten son, the Personification of Love, that whosoever believed in the Personification of Love would not perish but have everlasting life.* Continuing the substitution with verses 17 and 18: *For the Totality of Love sent the Personification of Love into the world, not to condemn the world, but that the world through Him, the Personification of Love, might be saved. 18: He who believes in the Personification of Love, is not condemned; but he who does not believe is condemned already because he has not believed in the name of the only begotten son, the Personification of Love, of the Totality of Love.*

John Calvin used the words "condemned already" in verse 18 to support his doctrine of predestination, specifically that before a person is born it has been predetermined whether the individual is saved and bound for heaven or has been condemned to hell. The doctrine holds that the individual's life is but a reflection of what has been ordained by God. This is synonymous with the concept of "fate," or "It is written in the stars." The Indo-Europeans, both the Greeks and the Indians, believed in fate. The oracle of Delphi and the great Indian epic of *Mahabharata* attests to this belief. A firm belief in fate undoubtedly helped the Indo-Europeans to be fearless warriors. "It is not the risks I take or the enemy's actions that determine whether I die today; it is fate."

My questions about salvation were partially answered: they are discoverable. Perhaps more importantly, many of those questions dropped out of importance. We really don't know what salvation is or how to get there, but we do know what the good, just, and loving life looks and feels like. It is here now. That is more than ample reason to live one's life abiding with those principles.

My most important question had become: "How big is one's circle of people to which each of us applies these principles? Are they to be applied only to myself, or just to my family, my community, my clan, my country, or to all of humankind?" My answer is: to all of humanity.

So, I have a god, not in the conventional sense of a supernatural anthropomorphic being who interacts with people and events in the world, but a god of the spirit of human love that (not who) goes unrecognized by man, or at least most. Many people would consider me an atheist; I do not mind that designation.

In my religious-group studies, I did not see karma and reincarnation as essential parts of Hinduism or Buddhism, and these teachings were not present in Confucianism or Taoism. Judaism, Christianity, and Islam are also ethical religions, but the circle of inclusion is smaller. It is not universal.

In Joshua's time a whole army was punished because one warrior disobeyed the Lord and Joshua by taking loot from killed enemies for himself rather than taking it to the Lord's warehouse.

In launching the Crusades, Pope Urban II said it was okay to kill Muslims, that the Commandment against killing did not apply, and he gave absolution for "sins" committed on the battlefield. The Inquisitions were devoid of love or benevolent considerations. After 9/11 even the United States resorted to torture for the interrogation of prisoners. Need and desire to win the war caused us to violate our own values. In this regard, the enemy has already won. "How big is your circle of concern for others?" became *the* abiding question for me.

For me this news brought sharp relief to the issue of the god whose actions are for the individual and the so-called god of history, whose actions have a much wider purpose, e.g.: the Babylonian captivity. The "god of history" is a phrase I had not fully appreciated previously. So God had two motivating forces on him: the effects on the individual, and the effect on society and history. Six-million Jews killed along with five-million "undesirables"—criminals, mentally ill people, homosexuals, and others. To me, there was no justice in any part of this. I could not imagine any aim or purpose that could be motivating God. It was simply the action of an evil madman who had acquired enormous power.

The United Nations partitioned Palestine. This displaced people whose ancestors had lived on that land for over 2,000 years—and without any pretense of compensation. This was not the dawning of a new day, a new age of justice in the world!

State Hospital

One of our last courses in medical school that academic year covered physical diagnosis. Several summer jobs were available, doing physical examinations on in-patients in the state mental hospital at Columbia, 110 miles away. The pay would cover my tuition for the year. If any of us found anything that was abnormal or that we were not sure of, we were to notify the senior staff for them to check it out. I wanted to be good at physical examinations. I did about 1,800 physicals that summer.

Those weeks or months were very happy for me. Med school was going well. I had a number of new insights into religions. It all made increasing sense. I somehow had the ability to quiet unruly patients in a matter of seconds, patients who would otherwise be given an injection and held or tied down until the drugs took effect.

Relationship Break-up

I still believed the religious differences between me and my Catholic sweetheart could be resolved easily. However, I did recognize that I needed some religious counsel. I called and scheduled a half-hour appointment with a priest who was covering while the regular priest was away. I arrived promptly at eight. By 1:00 a.m. we were sitting on his balcony overlooking the city of Columbus, drinking beer together. Ten days later, I called to make another appointment. The priest I had spoken with had left and another priest was covering. I made an appointment with him. Ten to fifteen minutes into the appointment, he was in tears. I was surprised and shocked. I had not foreseen that reaction even as a possibility. I backtracked. I said many of the things the first priest had told me. After about thirty minutes, the priest regained his composure. I left feeling terrible! I had diminished the man's faith. He undoubtedly had had some serious doubts before I arrived. I had not intended to do anything close to that. Still, I had hurt him, which I had no right to do. I reflected that this was the same lesson I thought I had learned as an evangelistic atheist during high school. I could not do anything like that to a woman I loved. I could not risk doing something like that to her. She had made her position clear in regard to eating beef publicly during a Friday dinner. I was beside myself.

Days grew into weeks. It was a classical conflict between desire and reason. I knew I had to let her go, but I couldn't act. My ardor waned. I recognized the inevitable outcome. I won't detail all the parameters of that struggle with myself or her responses. Finally one day, I called her for a date, and she informed me she was engaged. He was a college graduate of the class ahead of mine. He converted to Catholicism, and they were married.

I became despondent. In September, I wrote a poem. (See Exhibit C.) The work in med school was interesting, but my class standing for that year fell from middle third of the class to lower third.

Medical Studies Continued

In spite of my having earned my tuition, money was extremely tight, and Dad suffered a mild heart attack. Both of these added to my depression. I tried to join one of the career-incentive-for-physicians programs offered by the military. I was rejected due to my eyes.

Every day that year I spent fifty-two cents for breakfast, skipped lunch, and spent another fifty-seven cents for supper. Home visits dropped to once a month to do the books in my father's business. I did not date that academic year or the next. I would not date again until my internship.

At age 24 in the summer of 1957, I took the best-paying job in the medical field that I could find, a clerkship in psychiatry in the University Hospital. This began my financial independence, which provided immediate relief for my family. My sister Sallie started college that fall at Furman University in Greenville, South Carolina. Part of their relief was the realization that, in all likelihood, I wouldn't need to call on the family again.

We had one unusual patient that summer. A woman in her early thirties from the marshes south of Charleston was admitted because she was paralyzed from the waist down. All of her reflexes were normal. It was psychological paralysis. She said it happened at midnight. Someone had taken a small bundle of sticks, tied them together, smeared them with chicken blood, and thrown the bundle at her door, hitting it. "I knew what that meant," she said. "It meant I was *root worked*." That is, a voodoo spell had been put on her, and she was paralyzed. Her "friend" had done this to her because she'd had sexual intercourse with the friend's man. Our chief, Dr. Cleckley, told her that he was the greatest root doctor in these parts, and that he would return later in the afternoon to give her some medicine, and she would feel the hex leaving her right through her skin. "It will feel like your skin is on fire as it leaves your body, and the hex will be gone."

She said, "No, you ain't no root doctor. You can't do nothing for me; only the woman who hexed me can."

The chief reiterated that he could, and that he would remove her hex. Still she said she didn't believe it. A social worker talked to her about not doing things to get herself *root worked*. We returned about four hours later. Both the chief and the patient repeated their statements. Then he injected into her vein nicotinic acid, which created the sensation that the skin was very hot, "on fire." As he withdrew the needle, she screamed, "Oh, you is the greatest!" and she ran down the hall. The social worker saw her again to reinforce her earlier messages.

From the time I got that clerkship, I gradually recovered from my grief and depression.

For the 1957-58 school year, I and other senior medical students took jobs as externs at a private Catholic hospital, St. Francis. We took detailed patient histories and did admitting physical exams. Another senior, George Campbell, and I were roommates at St. Francis.

We were oriented by the chief of the medical staff, then by the Mother Superior. Among other things she told us was that if a woman comes in who has passed a blood clot vaginally, it might be a miscarriage. We were to treat it as though it was. We were to sprinkle water on the clot and say, "I baptize thee in the name of the Father, the Son, and the Holy Ghost," then make a sign of the cross over the clot. She said it made no difference who we were or what our religion was. She went on to say that if the clot was the product of conception the child had been saved, and if it was only a blood clot, then no harm had been done.

From September to mid-June, working a fifth of the evenings and weekends, I had only one occasion to do so. A woman and her husband came in with a pair of bloody panties that showed evidence of a blood clot. She did not seem to be in any distress. I followed the procedure as instructed by the Mother Superior. When they were leaving, I looked at the couple; they both smiled and thanked me. The woman declined my offer to call her obstetrician. They had come in only for the baptism. Presumably, either of them could have performed the baptism.

The other three externs were married and lived at home. George and I lived in a large room on the 3rd floor of the hospital. Unlike the others, we slept in the same beds each night, on call or not.

The telephone was in the hall outside our room. Most of the time when we were not on call, George and I could sleep through a number of rings. Once when I was not on call, the phone rang and rang. The next night I remarked to Henney, the night switchboard operator, "You must have to ring the phone a lot to get a response from George or me." She said, "No, both of you are fairly prompt." This meant that George and I could pre-set our minds to be awakened quickly if we were on call and not if we weren't on call.

For years I had been able to set my mind to awaken at a specified time in the future. This is similar to how a mother can set her mind to awaken to the sound of her child's cry. But I had not known this "setting" could be changed every night at will. George and I were also roommates during our internship year at City Hospital in St. Louis. The same thing happened that year with only the single phone in our room.

Often at 11:00 p.m. or so, I walked half a mile to Colonial Lake, a standard city block with an underground connection to the sea of Charleston Harbor. I often walked around the lake several times, reciting poetry. *Invictus*[8] by William Henley gave me determination and stamina, *Abou Ben Adhem* by James Henry

Leigh Hunt, and the first part of *Annabel Lee* by Edgar Allan Poe were my favorites during this period. I thought of *Annabel Lee*'s "high borne kinsmen who took her from me" as the Catholic Church and community. In place of the "cold wind from the north chilling and killing my Annabel Lee," I substituted "killing her love for me." *Invictus* was the poem that helped Nelson Mandela during his 27-year imprisonment in South Africa.

Invictus
By William Ernest Henley

Out of the night that covers me,
    Black as the Pit from pole to pole,
I thank whatever gods may be
    For my unconquerable soul.

In the fell clutch of circumstance
    I have not winced nor cried aloud.
Under the bludgeonings of chance
My head is bloody, but unbowed.

Beyond this place of wrath and tears
    Looms but the horror of the shade,
And yet the menace of the years
    Finds, and shall find me, unafraid.

It matters not how strait the gate,
    How charged with punishments the scroll,
I am the master of my fate;
    I am the captain of my soul.

For me the saddest poem is *Her Letter* by Robert Service.[9]

After Medical School

I graduated from Medical College of South Carolina in June 1958. I decided on four requirements for my internship: It had to be a hospital in which the interns had first-line responsibility, it had to be associated with a medical school, it had to be a rotating internship, and it had to pay a stipend I could live on. These criteria were met by St. Louis City Hospital with attending staff from Barnes Hospital, part of the Washington University. I learned a great deal. On the internal medical service, another intern and I had a sixty-bed ward under the supervision of a resident and the attending physician. About half of our sixty patients had a psychiatric problem, either as the cause or as a major contributing factor. This experience plus other reasons convinced me to go into psychiatry. Dr. Kenneth Apple of the University of Pennsylvania had been writing articles on religion and psychiatry. I visited that program and others. However, at the University of Pennsylvania the first of three years was in a state hospital several miles away. I had had state hospital experience. At length, I concluded that the best psychiatry residency for me was at the University of Michigan. The options were wide open. One was to take graduate-level courses with other graduate students. I took Religions of the Ancient Near East and an Anthropology course, selecting these in larger part on the reputation of the professors. Both courses were superb. They broadened my understanding of so-called primitive religions. I have continued to read these topics.

In my psychiatric training, my second rotation was in child psychiatry. Later I would take a Child Psychiatry residency, and be credited with this rotation.

As a resident in child psychiatry, I received a consultation request from Dr. Paul Ertel, who was a pediatric resident. A pre-teen patient on the pediatric ward had started menstruating without any advance knowledge. I suggested they have one of their nurses educate her. I was told that none of the nursing staff were willing to do this. This was the early 1960s, a time when even professionals often did not feel comfortable talking about such subjects. I told them to get a savvy nurse to work with me *stat*—the medical term for "without delay"—and we would enlighten the girl.

Talking with the patient, I used terms like "menstrual blood flow," and the nurse picked right up in a natural manner. She did a very good job answering the girl's questions. When I congratulated the nurse afterward, she beamed. I asked if she thought she could do it alone the next time. When she said, "Yes," I told her I thought she would not have any difficulty at all, but that I would be available.

I had not used psychiatric jargon. Dr. Paul Ertel was impressed. He invited me to his home. This began a friendship of many years.

Paul could be playful and silly as well as serious. My life up to this point had been very serious. It was not surprising that I was a serious fellow. From being around Paul, I saw how to play better. I volunteered to help him in clearing some brush from his land. This brought me a sense of nostalgia. I had cleared a lot of brush as a teen on the fifteen acres Dad had bought. Paul and I would have non-exploding bottle-rocket fights. The rockets traveled about 100 yards in roughly the direction aimed. We used pipe designed to hold electrical wire, conduit. This ended when our source stopped selling non-exploding bottle rockets.

During my psychiatric training, I was granted a year's rotation at the Mental Health Research Institute at the university. This was cut to nine months with minimal notice because an experienced senior resident was leaving to go to California, and the administration felt they needed someone with experience to replace him.

I had been attempting to identify emotions on the basis of the physics of sound in the spoken voice. I believed that just by hearing someone over the telephone, even in a foreign language, a number of emotions could be identified. There would have to be trials by parents and teachers to establish reliability. I was also extending this to verbal sounds toddlers make. Cutting my rotation short precluded me from coming to any plans or conclusions about feasibility or how best to proceed. That would have to be a different lifetime.

During my child psychiatry residency, I consulted at three different school systems: the Ann Arbor Public Schools, the Wayne-Westland School District, and the University School.

Mother's Birthday

My mother's sixtieth birthday was February 1960. I wrote a poem for the occasion. (See Exhibit D.) It is my favorite of the poems I have written. When Peggy recently read this poem, she asked, "How could you write something that loving after your experience with her and the aftermath in regard to your grandmother's accusation that you stole her money?" My answer had several components.

She is my mother. She did love me. My grandmother's dementia was in its early stages and was not generally recognized.

Somehow my hurts never turned to anger. Perhaps the poem is saying the same thing in different words.

My grandmother was always Queen Bee. Her father owned a plantation on Albemarle Sound in Gates County, North Carolina. He was the only one of my ancestors to have slaves, to my knowledge. My grandmother's role in the household was to entertain company and to look pretty. It was her sisters' lot to do the work of preparation for entertaining. This pattern continued throughout their lives and through the next generation.

My aunt TT did the entertaining, and my mother did the work of preparation. My aunt was sent to Europe for a time. It was Mother and her father who had the bulk of the chores. (My aunt confirms this.)

My grandmother was something of a flirt. She was thirteen years older than her husband. He came to fill a religious position at the school her father ran at Reynoldson, North Carolina.

My grandfather was a quiet, patient man. My grandmother's most common expression to her husband was, "Daddy, step & fetch it." Throughout her life the world revolved around her. She also had the status of being "somewhat holy" because two of her brothers and her husband were ministers. These attitudes were inculcated in my mother growing up.

The point here is that no one questioned or challenged the Queen Bee. I knew all of this from before the age of ten.

Her husband (my grandfather) had died in August 1943. The theft accusation occurred two to four months later.

One important lesson I learned for life was "Don't hold a grudge; it only hurts you." I don't know when or how I learned this principle. I do know it has been an abiding principle. I think it has served me well.

There was no one else I could relate to or count on. This was obvious to me then, and even more when Dad threatened to banish me at age twelve.

Over the years of my late teens and twenties, an alliance grew between my mother and me. Dad's illness and hospitalization, and the fact that money from the locker club came primarily on my shift, encroached on Dad's position. I was aware of it during those years, but saw no way to change it.

After my internship, I drove to Michigan from St. Louis in my Anglia, a small British Ford, arriving to start work as a psychiatric resident at age 26 on July 1, 1959. One of the things I did shortly after my arrival was to take instruction in Buddhism. Among other things, I was assigned a mantra, a two-syllable word that had no inherent meaning. The goal was to clear the mind to make it empty. I learned to do so, but found no benefit to it. I stopped shortly after that, but found it helpful in 1997 for a different purpose after my cardiac surgery, which I will discuss in the section titled "Post-op Recovery."

Courtship

Overview:

At age 26 in January 1960, I met senior medical student Marguerite Christine Raft—"Peggy." In late April, I proposed marriage. She turned me down flat—twice. She said "Yes" in October. Together we went to her minister to ask him to perform the ceremony. A few sentences into our request, the minister changed the subject—asking Peggy what to take for his cold. I walked away.

We married on June 24, 1961, in Maryland, across the state line from Washington, D.C. We have three adult children, and are very proud of each one. We also had a premature infant who lived only twenty-two hours.

We joined the Bushnell Congregationalist Church (The United Church of Christ) in Detroit, Michigan. It was relatively close to our home. Peggy's family had been members there while she was in grade school. We knew we wanted children, and we wanted them to have a religious education. I made a sincere effort to become part of a Christian community. I volunteered to teach Sunday school for twelve-year-olds. I enjoyed the students but had trouble with the church-supplied syllabus. I could not believe the supernatural stories I was teaching. I recognized the hypocrisy of this situation and discussed it with Reverend Straight, who was in charge of religious education. He asked me to continue for a few weeks; then I was relieved.

Falling for Peggy

The first time I noticed Peggy, I was eating lunch in the hospital cafeteria when I saw two women, senior medical students. I watched them as they crossed the floor and took seats at the other end of my table. Peggy was extremely attractive to me, and I liked how she had a serious-yet-nonchalant attitude about her at the same time. I knew I had to talk with her! The first thing I had to do was get rid of my lunch companion. He was not intuitive at all, so somehow I excused myself, picked up my tray, and moved into the vacant seat next to Peggy just as a friend of mine sat down opposite me. Peggy glanced over at me and continued her conversation. I carried on a conversation with my friend while eavesdropping on Peggy's. I read Peggy's name from her clinical coat: "M.C. Raft." They were preparing for a Clinical Pathological Conference later in the afternoon. It soon became apparent that the case they were discussing was one of carcinoma of the esophagus. I interrupted their conversation, telling them that the incidence of carcinoma of the esophagus was highest in China, and in the United States it was highest in New Orleans, followed by Charleston, South Carolina. I told them that speculation was that the incidence was thought to be extremely hot tea, all of which was true, but some people suspected the cause was eating corn pone. Having delivered the smoothest ice-breaker in the history of dating, I excused myself and left.

That evening, I looked for her phone number, but it wasn't in the phone book. I looked in the student directory—not there, either. Could I have misread her name? In the library I checked the annual and verified her picture and name. I reverted to a strategy I had used in college. I went to the librarian and asked,

"If someone had a book out that you needed to call in, and you had no phone number, how would you locate the student?" People used to be quite willing to give out information when they sensed romance, at least in those years. The librarian suggested the student directory. I said it wasn't there. She had only one thing to offer when I pressed her: "Call the dean's office."

That Saturday afternoon I sat reading in my office. I couldn't call the dean's office for a woman's phone number. I put the idea out of my mind, but it would not stay out of my mind. Taking the hospital phone book out of my desk, I looked up the dean's number and wrote it down. Thinking how inappropriate such a call would be, I decided to come up with some other way to get her number. I guessed which hospital ward she might be assigned to. Two or three such calls left me still in the dark. Then almost without thinking I dialed the dean's number, even though it was a Saturday afternoon.

"Hello." (Not very professional for a dean's office, I thought.)

"This is Dr. Marshall Shearer; I am trying to get in touch with a senior medical student, M.C. Raft. I wonder if you could help me." I fully expected the other party to identify himself as a custodian, but why would the custodial service answer the phone? Maybe he thought it was one of his children calling.

"Hello, Marshall. This is Dr. Waldo Bird," said the Associate Dean and Professor of Psychiatry who had interviewed me when I applied to the residency program.

I thought, What to do now?

After another, "How are you?" or some such, he said, "Just a minute; I'll see if I can get that information for you." He was back on the phone momentarily. "All I could find was a Marguerite C. Raft."

"M.C. Raft. Marguerite C. Raft. That would fit, wouldn't it?"

He said, "Yes, I guess it would."

I could tell by the change in the sound of his voice that he understood thoroughly. He gave me the number and said, "Would you like the address, too?"

I said, "Well, sir, since you have it right there, yes."

The three of us talked about it months later; we were all quite pleased with the outcome.

I called her the next Tuesday evening. "This is Doctor Marshall Shearer. Did people of the pathological conference think the patient's esophageal cancer was due to corn pone?" She picked right up on my question. After chatting a moment or two, I asked her to go out with me sometime that weekend. This gave her the options of Friday evening, Saturday all day and evening, and the same on Sunday. It was a technique I had used at college. If the woman said, "No," I would have moved on. Peggy gave me a blanket turn-down but continued to talk and be friendly.

Monday of the following week we had a nice conversation, except that her turn-down included, "I'm working." However, few jobs do not allow time off. I tolerated the ambiguity. I did not call her the next week. A week later, I did call her. "There is a Gilbert and Sullivan play this weekend at the Lydia Mendelssohn Theatre; do you want to go with me or not?" I was surprised when she said, "Yes." Although the theater was just across the street from her rooming house, I picked her up in my Anglia. At the time, I didn't realize how important this fact would be. As we were driving, she asked which medical department I was in. When I told her psychiatry, I saw her instinctively move back against her seat, then look at the speedometer and then out the window. Later she acknowledged that she was thinking of fleeing, but decided that she couldn't make it in high heels at our speed. She just hoped no one would recognize her and realize she was out with a psychiatrist!

We enjoyed the performance. The play was *Ioloantha*. In the opening scene, two men came on stage in tights with curled up toes, singing, "We are dainty little fairies." During the play we frequently looked at each other at poignant moments. After the play, as she got in the car, I asked if she would prefer to go to a milk bar or to go get a beer. She said we didn't need to do that; I could just take her home.

I said, "Not yet."

She asked, "Where would we go for the beer?"

I said, "The Old German, a restaurant and bar," and turned in that direction. My question about the milk bar was in case she didn't drink and objected to going to a bar. She took it as an indication of naiveté. She was afraid she was leading me astray. As we were moving to a table inside the bar, several patrons and waitresses sailing by with trays loaded with beer spoke to me, calling me by name. Her fears of leading me astray were eliminated. We ordered a pitcher of beer, and other patrons gave us two half-pitchers as they left. It was a great evening.

We continued to date. I decided to go home to South Carolina for Easter. There I walked the railroad tracks, my thinking place of old; I also went to the beach, sometimes alone, other times with a family member. The weather was cold, in the fifties. The sea was rough with waves and wind, but the view was grand—Mother Nature. On the beach I picked up a number of sand dollars and wrapped each in tissue paper. While in South Carolina, I decided I wanted to marry Marguerite C. Raft. On the way out of town, I bought a purse made of woven marsh grass from a roadside vendor. I headed back to Michigan.

I presented Peggy with the purse "full of dollars" on our first date after my return. She protested, "I can't accept that." At length, I persuaded her to look inside the purse. With some trepidation she did. Her expression showed a definite sense of relief, and she happily accepted. Soon thereafter, I proposed. She replied that marriage was not part of her plans. "My roommate Molly is into that; you could ask her." I told her I was only interested in marrying *her*. Her plans were to finish her medical training, return to her hometown, and become a partner with the talented family physician she had worked for since her sophomore year in college, Dr. Robert Heart. Her mother would run her office, which would put her at the hub of information, and Link Huber would take care of the cattle and horses she hoped to buy. She already owned a kennel of collies and had owned a horse since the ninth grade. Besides, she said she had never known of a marriage which she felt significantly added to the happiness of the couple. Her "No" was emphatic. I took it that way.

She graduated in early June and left for her internship in Washington, D.C. After some weeks, I wrote her, "I told you I would give you my aunt and uncle's address in Virginia; here it is…" She replied with a four-page newsy letter. We wrote.

My brother was a midshipman at the Naval Academy, which was holding an open house in September. My parents and my siblings were going. I arranged to go to Washington to see Peggy a week later. My aunt invited her to spend the weekend at their home. Dad was hurt and somewhat angry that I valued "that damn girl" over being with the family.

I took Peggy a gift wrapped in tissue paper with a ribbon and presented it to her in front of my aunt and uncle. Again Peggy protested, "I can't accept this" and on and on. At length, she agreed to "just look at it." Opening it, she saw an empty jar with a screw top. I explained it was a jar of Michigan air. "Thought you might be getting homesick for a breath of Michigan air." The weekend went well and was enjoyable.

I had been selected by the psychiatry department to take a grant from the federal government for three weeks' special training in mental retardation at Letchworth Village in Thiels, New York, thirty or so miles up the Hudson River from New York City. Peggy planned to drive for an interview for a residency in New Jersey, then pick me up later in the day, and we would drive to my aunt and uncle's house for the balance of the weekend. Driving to Washington through Delaware, we stopped to eat. We were just sitting in the car, necking. A presidential debate between Nixon and Kennedy was on the radio when she said, "I will be disappointing a lot of people, but I will marry you." The date was October 7, 1960.

The next Monday I sent her a dozen long-stemmed red roses. When she told Molly about the flowers, Molly not only knew who had sent them, but she also recognized their significance—that we were engaged.

Peggy made two trips back to Michigan that year. One was on Armistice Day, the other a two-week vacation in February. She had told her family that we were engaged. Peggy had two brothers: Greg, who was three years older than Peggy; and Byron, two years older. That first night they took us to a striptease show. I also met her Aunt Helen, her mother's only sibling, and her Uncle Ivan.

I had arranged to borrow a car for the eighty-mile drive to Peck, Michigan, where her mother was a Justice of the Peace. When we reached the county line, I pulled over to let Peggy drive to eliminate the risk of my having to appear before her mother. (I had heard enough stories about her.) Upon arrival I received a cool, but cordial reception. Nothing was said about our relationship until Greg arrived in the afternoon. He took me to the hotel bar where we had a good discussion. Later in the afternoon, Peggy's mother had ten of her women friends over to meet me. I was introduced to all ten, one right after another. I don't know how I did it, but I recalled each woman's name and used each name when we parted.

That year I flew to Washington, D.C., to see Peggy about every third weekend.

On her vacation, among her relatives, her friends, and my friends, we had ten cocktail parties during those two weeks. My best man, Fari Amini, was a fellow resident. We had both been skeptical about some of the theories we were being taught. Other residents seemed to take everything in faith by authority. Fari was a Muslim from Tehran, Iran, a proud man. Our party at his house was on day ten. Alcohol was plentiful. Not to drink at his party would have been taken as disrespectful, even after a lot of explanation. I went into the kitchen and made myself a "martini" with only water and an onion. Fari saw me and said, "You don't drink martinis. What gives?"

I said, "This is a special occasion. I thought I would try something different." I found Peggy and offered her a taste of my drink. She politely declined. I persisted. She realized I didn't drink martinis and that I could accept a "No," so at length she tasted it and recognized it was water, said it was good, and asked if she could have one just like it. I told her to keep that one; I would get another.

On that trip to Michigan, we went to her clergyman in the United Church of Christ and asked him to perform our wedding ceremony. He may have said a short "Yes," but then changed the subject by asking Peggy what he could do for his cold. I walked away. Peggy decided we should get married in Washington, D.C. It would be roughly equal distance for both families in Michigan and South Carolina, and she could also maintain control over the proceedings much easier. The church was on the west side of West Moreland Circle in Maryland. We went to hear Reverend Dick preach, then to our appointment with him. When he learned we had heard the sermon that morning, he asked what we thought of it. I saw Peggy cringe. I answered honestly. That created a deeper bond between Reverend Dick and us. Several days later, Peggy went to Rockville and obtained the marriage license.

We were married June 24, 1961, the start of a wonderful new adventure. The reception was at Normandie Farms in Maryland. Our families had an hour to mingle, getting to know each other a bit. When we left the reception, we spent the first night in Williamsburg, Virginia. During the drive, I said, "You know, I never asked you if you could cook." She replied, "My horses love my hot bran mash."

Peggy had a year's residency in internal medicine lined up at Wayne County General Hospital in Michigan. I continued at the University of Michigan. I had rented a house roughly halfway between the two hospitals. Peggy took her second year of residency split between surgery and obstetrics. We settled into married life and our routines, and lived there three years.

Paul Ertel

Peggy and I became good friends with Paul and Inta Ertel.

Our families spent social time together, visiting each other's homes, sliding down the hill covered with snow, and watching their two girls and our three children play. We took trips and vacations together.

New Year's Eve parties lasting until the wee hours became a standard. Our large house could seat 35 in the dining room with its large fireplace. The men would wear tuxes, the women long skirts sewn to the bottoms of their dresses. For several years, Paul dressed as Father Time while I appeared as the New Year, sporting a baby's cap, white string as tie with undershirt, a sheet for a diaper, and white socks. One New Year's, Paul carried a snow saucer to the top of a large hill and lit the fuse of a Roman candle, then pushed off, yelling and firing all the way down. Unfortunately, the hill was in the horse pasture, and near the bottom Paul's saucer hit a pile of frozen horse dung, spilling Paul and tearing his tux. I was with him when he took it to the tailor and asked, "You menda these?" The tailor responded, "You rippadease?" Paul often fed other people such straight lines.

In warm weather we would float down the Huron River in an old Sears aluminum flat-bottom boat with square bow and a steering oar in the rear. We would cook hot dogs and burgers on the Hibachi while drinking beer.

After Paul and his family moved to Columbus, we visited several times. One trip stands out: Our youngest was five months old and throwing up often. This apparently influenced the Ertels not to have a third child. I always felt bad about this, as our third, Tom, has given us so much joy.

Trying Another Church

After my unsatisfying attempt to teach sixth-grade Sunday school at Bushnell, I made another effort to become a religious person prior to September 1983. This attempt focused on the Ann Arbor United Church of Christ. Peggy's brother and his wife attended church there, and I admired the heritage of Reverend Lloyd Douglas and his book *The Magnificent Obsession*. Peggy and I would sit in the pews, and if the minister was saying something I strongly disagreed with, I would become fidgety. This disturbed Peggy and probably others. Equally distasteful for Peggy were my explanations afterwards. After several months we stopped going to church.

Terry Tice

A year or so after Peggy and I married, I met Terry Tice, who held a PhD degree in theology from Princeton University and a PhD in philosophy from the University of Michigan. Terry had run an advertisement in the newspaper for a course he was to teach on Harvey Cox's *Secular City*. I was impressed by Terry. At length our families became close friends.

When our daughter Millie was four years old, she and Jonathan Tice, Terry and Carol Tice's son, also four, got inside the locked swimming-pool fence and into the water. They got themselves out. We had a great swimming hole 800 feet away down at the river, so I took a sledge hammer and broke a good-sized hole in the bottom of the pool. It would no longer hold water. All four parents were relieved. Later, the swimming pool was filled in and covered with topsoil. It is now the site of our garden.

Over the years, Terry and I have had many talks about many issues in religion.

When Terry retired from the University of Michigan, he moved to Colorado. When I started to work on *Toward Interfaith Harmony* in earnest, I spent four days with him and, subsequently, had many phone conversations. He helped me tremendously. (See the Acknowledgments in *Harmony*.)

Millie

On September 12, 1963, Peggy delivered Mildred Helen Shearer (Millie) two weeks late. With reddish hair, Millie was an exceptionally beautiful baby, at least in her father's eyes. Millie was named for her paternal grandmother, Mildred, and for Peggy's mother's sister, Aunt Helen.

At an intersection on the way home from the hospital after Millie's birth, I told Peggy that I saw three stop signs. In a joking tone she responded, "With only one eye, you are not supposed to be able to see double. How do you get to three?" I had developed a cataract on my eye. Its multiple layers produced the three images.

We had made one exploratory trip looking at faculty positions in child psychiatry to begin the following summer. I was offered a position at the University of Michigan as instructor, and I accepted. Peggy and I would drop Millie at a babysitter's on our way to the campus. Peggy would go to the Student Health Service while I walked to the Children's Psychiatric Hospital. We rode home together, picking up Millie on the way.

Millie was a happy child, but had a temper. She excelled in school. Peggy and I required all of our children to take band through the tenth grade. Other than sports, band was the only place cooperation was taught in her school.

In high school, Millie had the lead female role in the production of *South Pacific*. She attended Kalamazoo College in Kalamazoo, Michigan. There she had the lead role playing Joan of Arc in *The Lark*. After college she took a year at Rutgers toward a Masters in Fine Arts. She did not return for the second year. Instead, she began trying out for parts in various productions. She supported herself by doing editorial work at night.

She enrolled in an advertised course about the financial aspects of an acting career taught by Gerry Goodman. She had conversations with him after class. He invited her to visit the New York Morehouse, a modern-day commune in Manhattan. The founder of Morehouse had devised a governing system that was successful; it gave everyone equal veto power over proposed changes. Most communes had failed over governing issues. His solution was simple: Every member could stop any change just by voting "no." Abstentions were tolerated.

The mission of the house was to serve the world unselfishly and make a profit. As a group they did quite a bit to feed the homeless, collecting donated foods, repackaging the food into individual-sized portions, and distributing it in homeless-populated sections of New York City.

Millie moved out of the rooming house foyer she had been living in, and moved into the Morehouse. They also had houses in Atlanta, Georgia, and Lafayette, California. There were about fifteen people living in the house when Millie joined. One man, Jonathan Gross, was Jewish. Within six months, he and Millie had fallen in love. Neither set of parents were happy with their prospects. Complicating matters further, many of Jonathan's parents' friends were conservative Jews, and Millie had set the wedding date on the Sabbath between Rosh Hashanah and Yom Kippur. Jonathan was so love-struck that he wouldn't stand up to Millie. I don't think he even tried to explain how Jonathan's parents and friends would be offended.

Peggy and I flew to New York City to meet Jonathan's parents, David and Sylvia Gross, and to see Millie and Jonathan. David was a retired orthodontist. The six of us met in a restaurant. I would guess it was Sylvia who stated the problem of having the wedding on the Sabbath. I told Millie she couldn't do that, she didn't realize what she was proposing, it would be an insult to every one of his parents' friends, the Sabbath was sacred, and conservative Jews were not supposed to ride in a car on the Sabbath. Further, I pointed out that she had planned the wedding to take place on the estate of one of her parents' friends in Pennsylvania, which would require car transportation. And still further, the Sabbath between Rosh Hashanah and Yom Kippur is a time for self-evaluation and to make amends.

I also told Millie that if she converted to Judaism, she would have our blessing, even though she probably wouldn't think of us in that regard. She said she had no intention of converting. I said that is true now, but with children you might want more family solidarity.

I asked Jonathan's parents if they needed to correct anything I had said or add to it. They didn't.

The wedding was rescheduled for September 6, 1992. It was a beautiful day. Millie and Jonathan had arranged for both a Presbyterian minister, Reverend Paul Smith of Brooklyn, who happened to be black; and a white female Rabbi, Julie Greenberg of Philadelphia. Although these two clergy had not worked together before, they worked hand in glove. Millie and Jonathan wrote their own vows. They each thanked the other's parents for their spouse.

After the wedding, one of David Gross's friends came up to me and said, "We count you as one of us." That is one of the best compliments I have ever received.

I was significantly concerned about the lack of balance in power in their relationship. Jonathan would not stand up to Millie. After about a year and a half, he began to do so. Millie reacted by driving from New York City to see us. She and Peggy talked. The power shift had occurred. I felt the marriage now had a chance to continue to grow.

Father's Death

My father died May 3, 1964, of congestive heart failure; and judging by the pain he complained of, he also had a heart attack. When I had seen him the summer before, I recognized the symptoms of heart failure and sent him to Dr. Ford Rivers, a cardiologist who had been my chief resident in medical school. Dr. Rivers digitalized Dad, resulting in dramatic improvement. After several months, Dad thought he no longer needed the medicine. Without talking to Dr. Rivers or me, he stopped taking the Digitalis. Soon he was in heart failure again. He returned to Dr. Rivers, but died before he was completely digitalized again. We had not expected that his death was imminent. I feel both sad and angry at Dad over his death. He left a fair number of poems and short stories unfinished. Mother, my sister Sallie, and I spent several days trying to salvage what we could. We had a private printing done of his writings. He had gotten to see and hold Millie the previous Christmas, to his great delight.

Memorial services were held in North Charleston, South Carolina, and Lincolnton, North Carolina, where Dad was buried with my mother's parents and my brothers. The women of the North Charleston church came up to Mother, embraced her, and cried. I was concerned about the emotional strain on her. My own grief vanished as I thought about the strain on my mother, but returned when I concluded my assessment. Although I was prepared to intervene to spare her, it was never necessary.

As I was about to enter the church for Dad's memorial service in North Charleston, Isaac Campbell spoke to me. I took Isaac by the arm and we entered the church together. He sat with our family. He may well have been the first black person to attend a service there.

I postponed allowing myself to experience the full force of my grief for about a month. Then I took a day off. With no one else in the house, I wrote and I cried for two-thirds of the day. I polished that writing later: "My Father Has Embarked." (See Exhibit E.)

My Legal Blindness

For five years, 1963-68, I was legally blind secondary to the cataract. I could not see to drive. I resigned from consulting one day a week for the Michigan Department of Corrections and the Ann Arbor Public Schools. I sold my car. I read with books about an inch from my nose. I was told that after the cataract was removed, since the vitreous humour—the quasi fluid in the posterior chamber of the eye—was liquefied, I was not to do anything more strenuous than "lift a beer bottle for fear of causing a detached retina." I was an active person, so that restriction seemed crushing. I put off the surgery as long as possible, continuing to teach and supervise psychiatric residents. I could see that a person was there, but could not identify him or her by sight. I recognized people by the sound of their voices.

I had a Dictaphone and made voice notes with it. The styles of men's haircuts changed while I was blind. Also, I had formed a mental picture of people I had met while blind.

During this period of blindness, my mother offered to give me one of her eyes to be transplanted into my eye socket. I thanked her for her love and told her medical sciences couldn't splice the optic nerve.

During this period, I wrote a scientific article, "Periodic Organic Psychosis Associated with Recurrent Herpes Simplex," published with Stewart M. Finch, MD, who was head of the Child Psychiatry department. It was the lead article for its issue of *The New England Journal of Medicine*, 171; 494–497, September 1964. I tried to recover the virus from the spinal fluid of the patient. For these efforts I needed the cooperation of Dr. Vincent Hennessy, the head of a virus laboratory. In writing the manuscript, I tried to cover the issue from many different angles. When I took the manuscript to Dr. Hennessy, he told me to cut it in half and bring it back. I asked if he had read it. He said, "No," and repeated his directions. I did so. When I returned with half as many pages, he glanced at it and said, "Now cut it in half again, and I'll read it." I did. We were not successful in growing the virus from the cerebral-spinal fluid. I also wrote other articles in other scientific journals. I received a large number of requests for reprints of the article, "Why Children Steal." I have thirteen scientific articles published as lead author.

Our Own Home

Both Peggy and I wanted our own home. The potential complications of the cataract surgery were well known. I wanted to buy a house within walking distance of the hospital. Peggy wanted a place where she could keep horses, and she pointed out that we rode to and from work daily without any problems. Peggy had owned a horse since she was in ninth grade, and before that she often visited a riding stable about a mile from her home.

I told our real-estate agent, Mr. Bullard, that we would buy our house through him if it was listed. In the winter of 1964 he showed us 8044 Dexter-Pinckney Road. It was in a good school district. This home had been on the market for nine months. It needed a lot of repairs and improvements. There had been seven different owners in the past ten years. We closed on the property on March 30, 1964, and took possession on May 30.

The house had seven bedrooms, four on the third floor, but only one bathroom; there were still two outhouses behind the barn. The wiring consisted of exposed single-strand wire with two ceramic tubes where the wire went through a wall. The dishwasher overflowed the first night. It was plumbed with a plastic drain hose that ran uphill. When Peggy took a shower, the water ran downstairs into the kitchen. The barn had holes in the roof that one could throw a baseball through. There was a homemade swimming pool, with none of its corners square. The filtration unit had been left out all winter and frozen, breaking most of the pipes. The land was grossly overgrown. At one time the place had been fenced with wooden posts and three boards plus a cap board. Many of the posts were rotten. There was also a trash pile where owners had thrown TV dinner trays and cans, as well as an old mattress. Weekly trash pick-up cost four dollars a month. We picked up seven dumptruck loads of trash. Peggy would go to work and report "another day, another thousand dollars in the hole."

We started work on those tasks that would otherwise result in further deterioration. Our next priority was functions that we needed. I re-plumbed the entire house with Peggy's help. When I was putting in some new pipe, Peggy got scared noticing how close I put my face to the blowtorch to be able to see. She asked me to teach her how to do it. I did.

At one point I asked her to cut into one of the supply pipes (hot or cold), but to trace it out to be sure she didn't cut the wrong one. She did cut the wrong one, as announced by a spray of water from the cut. She would say later that she really felt loved that night when I didn't chew her out. I just fixed it.

We had rock wool insulation blown into the walls and ceiling.

The house had three small coal fireplaces and an oil furnace with radiator hot water. That fall when we fired up the furnace, we could feel the heat in the wall ten feet away from the chimney. We built a large wood fireplace and a two-flue chimney, one for the furnace. Every dime we could save or scrape together went into the house for six-plus years.

Chrissie

February 21, 1966, Christine Norma Shearer was born and named for her mother. She was extremely active even in utero. As she grew, she went directly from standing to running. Chrissie stood at nine months of age and began running at nine months three weeks. Early in her kindergarten year, she was the fastest runner in her class.

She was into horses before she started school. That love has continued. She graduated from Olivet College and took a masters degree in public administration from Eastern Michigan University. Currently she works for the Michigan Association of Health Plans.

Paul Ertel was the pediatrician for Millie and Chrissie, as well as for the premature child we lost. He did a great job, which was—is—very much appreciated.

Thomas's Birth

Thomas Gregory Shearer was born February 6, 1970.

As a toddler, our son, Thomas, was always into something. He examined the Great Dane's tonsils by extending his hand and arm into the dog's mouth. Or he would hide from the babysitter. She found him by listening for his laughter.

Tom took an associates degree from Ferris State College in architecture. He then went to Arizona State University to study solar architecture. However, Arizona would not give any credit for his studies at Ferris, in spite of his grades. He became bored, and went to work as a salesman for two years. He returned to Michigan and worked part time while he completed his Bachelor's degree at the University of Michigan-Dearborn. Currently he works as a salesman of strategic accounts for the Eastern half of the United States. Tom married Julie Dunville. They have two wonderful children.

Mending Fences

It was taking four to six weeks of all my free time each spring to replace, scrape, and paint fences. Then we discovered white PVC fencing. We installed the PVC in stages. My son-in-law Jonathan and I did 500 feet on the northern border. My son Tom, Chrissie's boyfriend, and I did 330 feet down the driveway. Tom and a friend did 390 feet across the front, and we hired to have most of the southern boundary done. At that time, installing PVC cost about one-and-a-half times new wood fencing, but the PVC needed minimal maintenance—no scraping, priming, or painting; just washing with a bleach solution and scrub brush.

Tom and I also installed an extensive irrigation system, drawing from the river. The material salesman tried to sell me an air compressor to blow the water out for the winter so it wouldn't freeze and burst the pipes. I told him, "I don't need it. I'll install it so the pipes will drain out by gravity." He told me I couldn't do it. I asked him why not. "Because," he said, "you can't find anyone reliable enough to install it with the proper pitch." I replied, "In this case, I can. All the work will be done by my son and me with a four-foot level. And we both know who will be repairing it if it isn't done right the first time." He said, "Good luck." We did install it properly, and it drains naturally every fall.

Our Horses

Peggy and I went to a horse auction in 1965 where she bought herself a "green broke" Arabian gelding for $500. On the same trip we bought me a "baby-sitter horse" for $300.

Peggy was quite excited when the horses were delivered. She got both of them bridled and saddled, then in an offhand way asked me if I knew which side to get on.

I replied, "Yes, any damn fool knows that."

She said, "OK, wise guy, which side?"

I said, "The top side, and I know the next thing I'm supposed to do."

She asked, "What's that?"

I said, "Stay there."

Peggy got mounted and had her horse move out a couple of steps. Because horses are herd animals that tend to stay together,

I had to hold my horse back. When Peggy noticed that we hadn't moved, she said, "Can't you make him go?"

I said, "I've only ridden on the merry-go-round. I'm waiting for the music to start. Could you hum a few bars?"

Hide and Seek

Every member of the family had a horse. We would ride together on horseback, and sometimes play hide & seek among the scrub trees on a large nearby tract of land. Some of our horses caught on to the game and would scrunch down to reduce their visibility. However, my horse would frequently whinny to the other horses as if to say, "Here I am."

At one point, Peggy thought we could raise horses and sell them when they were six to twelve months old. She acquired three nice brood mares. The foals were to sell for $750 to $2,000.

Just as our first crop of foals was ready, the market dropped for that type and price of horse.

A Spiritual Man

Peggy became good friends with one of her student patients, Judy Tishman, who also enjoyed horses. Judy arranged to board her horse, a tall Tennessee Walker, with us. She invited us to her parents' orchards in the western part of Michigan. Her father was one of the most remarkable men I have ever known. We spent some time talking; then he gave us a tour of his farm. I commented on his cherry trees, which appeared to be mature trees, even old trees; but most had roots that started six to nine inches from the base of a tree, came up four to six inches, then made almost a ninety-degree angle into the tree trunk. He explained that a cherry tree usually only lives thirty to thirty-five years. He said the trees in this orchard were over fifty. The circulation in these trees is vertical. He would watch his trees, and when one side of the tree began to fall behind, he planted a seedling right under the puny part. Later, he grafted the sprout into the tree.

Judy recounted the story of how one springtime, just as the cherries were in full bloom, a rain became a storm that knocked all the cherry blossoms from the trees. Her father watched the loss of his cherry crop from the window with equanimity. Then he turned and began playing chess.

Near the end of our visit he took us to "the sanctuary" on his farm. As we drove down a dirt road, he had Judy get out of the car to hold a large branch out of the way. We went down a well-kept hillside to a pond where all was quiet and serene. Instinctively, we spoke in low tones, if at all. We lingered there, absorbing the majesty of the place for some time. I was very impressed by this man's spirituality. I looked forward to spending more visits with him. Unfortunately, he died a few months later.

Children's Psychiatric Hospital

When I worked at Children's Psychiatric Hospital, there were three wards of sixteen patients each. Each patient had a resident psychiatrist assigned to him. All the patients on a ward were supervised by one of two faculty psychiatrists, one of whom was an instructor. The other was more experienced. I was an instructor.

Somehow I got it in my head that it would be good for the kids if they had a dog. It took time and persistence to get all the permissions from the head nurse, the hospital administration, and the Psychiatry Department for an adult male dog, not a puppy. I left the selection of the dog to Head Nurse Alice Williams, who obtained a German Shepard. He was a big hit with the kids. He was walked regularly. All went well until our male dog delivered a litter of puppies. The ward staff took it in stride. It was my resident doctors who had the most concern. "How do we explain to the patients about sex and birth and…?" The nurses had some difficulty, also, though not as much as the residents.

One of the ward staff, Elizabeth Yates, wrote a book about the experience: *Skeezer, Dog with a Mission, A True Account of a Canine Co-therapist Who Helps Emotionally Disturbed Children.*[10]

My Vision

In 1968, our family visited our friends Paul and Inta Ertel, who had moved to Dublin, Ohio. I helped Paul cut a walkable path down a steep ravine behind his house. On the drive back to Michigan, I noticed that part of my visual field was gray. The diagnosis was obvious: I had a detached retina behind the cataract. Surgery removed the cataract, followed by four weeks in bed with minimal exertion to prevent more of the retina from becoming detached, and to allow the surgical wound to heal. Then came the operation to repair my retina. Morton Cox, MD, who had been a classmate of Peggy's, did the surgery. The operation was successful. Because I had 5+ diopters correction for nearsightedness, I did not need thick corrective lenses with their disfiguring appearance, nor did I have the dreaded physical restrictions. I should have been joyful. In a way, I was. So why was I having suicidal thoughts?

I arranged to go into psychoanalysis with Dr. Arthur Miller. He had just come to the university from Chicago. He was a training analyst; that is, he trained others to be psychoanalysts. I was not interested in that, but I wanted a well-qualified analyst. I met with him four times a week for fifteen months. The essence of the analysis was Dad's fixation on my vision as well as Dad's tendency whenever we were feeling close to each other to say: "Both of your brothers were perfect physical specimens." He was trying to reassure both himself and me that there was nothing genetic in their deaths. I had been hearing the emotional message of closeness. Now I heard the implication of the words whose message was: "I wish one of them had lived instead of you." This message from Dad was a "double bind," as described by Gregory Batson. Dr. Batson reported a case of an adolescent boy who had been in a psychiatric hospital several weeks. He was judged to be ready for his first visit from his mother. When she came on the ward, she extended her arm with the hand upright—the "stop" position. She also turned her head away from him, but said, "Aren't you going to kiss me?" This insight about my father stopped my suicidal thoughts. It is a truism that before puberty most children would willingly die to secure a father's or mother's love.

I learned other things about myself in analysis. I left analysis with Dr. Miller's endorsement in order to join Masters and Johnson's Reproductive Biological Institute in St. Louis in 1970. (See the upcoming section "Masters and Johnson.")

Shortly after my eye surgery and my return to full activities and duties, Dean Hubbard of the medical school addressed each department. When he finished speaking, I stood and was recognized. "Dr. Hubbard, I need to be sure I understand you correctly. You have said that there will be no consideration for excellence in patient care or teaching or research unless the activity brings money into the medical school. Am I correct, sir?"

He replied, "Yes, that is the essence of it."

I thanked him and, as I sat down, I knew then that I would leave the med school.

Discovering Tillich

It was about this time that I first discovered the book *Ultimate Concern, Paul Tillich in Dialogue* by Professor McKinsey Brown. Tillich and Brown taught a twelve-session seminar for graduate students at the University of California at Santa Barbara in 1963, which was tape-recorded and transcribed, then edited by Dr. Tillich and subsequently published. I was initially attracted by the title. Tillich "spoke" to me.

Tillich addressed many issues and questions I had been contemplating, such as, Does the Ultimate shine through the finite or not? Some of his conclusions explained a lot: Love is the urge to unite with that which is loved. Self-love is necessary because otherwise the individual becomes very selfish. When a religion becomes fanatical, love is diverted away from humans and toward the cause. Religious symbols tend to ossify and become rigid. Tillich answered the question of what is our Ultimate Concern by concluding it ultimately means there is nothing further.

I had conversations with Terry Tice about the book and Tillich. Terry had been a student of Tillich's at the University of Chicago. Soon he had me reading Tillich's three-volume *Systemic Theology*. I read other books by Tillich and discussed them with Terry. It felt good to be simpatico with a major religious thinker.

Sex Talks at University

The university students' lack of knowledge about sexual subjects was both surprising and troublesome. My wife, Peggy, was working as a physician at the University of Michigan Student Health Service at the time. She knew of numerous coed students becoming pregnant without understanding the physiology, including several Phi Beta Kappa students who got pregnant and couldn't understand at all how it might have happened.

After a number of these reports, I told Peggy, "I'm tired of hearing about this; either do something about it, or keep it to yourself."

Two days later she said, "Okay, I'm ready to do something about it, but I need your help." Half joking, she added, "Now either help me or put up with my accounts."

She wanted to give sex-information talks with me, on invitation, to various housing units on invitation at the university. Because our own children were small, we limited these to one night per week.

The talks usually started with Peggy discussing the various types of contraception and their effectiveness rates. She identified the types that require a doctor's visit and prescription, along with the advantages and disadvantages of each method. In some states (e.g.: Connecticut) in the 1960s, it was illegal even to give out contraceptive *information*.

At the time, there was no legal way to terminate an unwanted pregnancy. Peggy described the stories she had heard from some of her patients who endured illegal abortions: being led blindfolded down alleys, not being allowed to bring a friend or family member for support. Some women reported smelling pipe smoke throughout the procedure. Several reported hearing vermin scurrying across the floor. While Peggy discouraged undergoing such a dangerous procedure, she stressed that any coeds who did, should come to the Student Health Service within 24 hours to be examined in an effort to detect post-operative infections early. These discussions established our credibility and allowed us to discuss relationships and values.

Peggy was also writing prescriptions for birth control. After about a year, she got a message, indirectly from the administration, to cease and desist. Legal age had recently been lowered from 21 to 18. As a result, the administration had dropped all house mothers in the residence halls and had allowed coed dorms, which saved the cost of house-mothers' salaries.

In a letter to the administration, Peggy pointed out how these changes left coeds without the common rationale many used to discourage young men from attempting to have intercourse. She pointed out the contradictions of their policy and their message to her. She said that if the administration would go back to house mothers and stop open visitations, she would be consistent with the new policy by not writing prescriptions for contraceptives. But she refused to be part of a "double policy" that punished young women with unwanted pregnancies. The university reverted to their prior practice of ignoring us. Some years later the administration asked if some representatives could attend a talk. We said "yes." Then the administration wanted to tape record some sessions. They made tapes of three: one talk to all women, one to all men, and one to a mixed audience.

Next they wanted to sponsor us, which would allow us to talk to audiences of 1,500 to 2,000 rather than the 100 to 150 we'd been speaking to. At our first big event, with microphones set up around the auditorium, Peggy was concerned about losing the informality and spontaneity of relating to the students as we had in their housing units. As Peggy, who was eight-months pregnant at the time, waddled up to the stage, I told the audience, "We will start the talk with contraception. Peggy is our expert on the subject. If that doesn't test our credibility, nothing we say will." The crowd erupted in laughter, and our concerns about losing the air of relaxed informality were settled.

Those three recordings were transcribed and ultimately published by Harper and Row as *Rapping About Sex* in 1972.[11]

Masters and Johnson

Dr. Ray Waggoner, chairman of the Department of Psychiatry at the University of Michigan was also a consultant with Masters and Johnson. He told Bill and Jenny about us, as a married medical couple who were comfortable talking about sex; furthermore, they were looking for a psychiatrist and an educator. They invited us to visit them in St. Louis at their expense to consider joining their staff as clinical and research associates. I told Dr. Masters that I would like to meet them, but that we were pretty well set, and the likelihood of our joining them was small. He said he would take that risk. We flew down for a long weekend. At that time, they audiotaped all therapy sessions with the patients' written permission.

They had us listen to a case. I made three pages of notes detailing what they were missing. At the end of their two-week stay, the patient couple was ecstatic with their success. On the second case, I took half a page of notes. These patients had the same result. For the third case, I didn't take any notes. Masters and Johnson had a superior treatment approach. We took a week's vacation to consider their offer.

The House Fire

On our first full day of that vacation, July 20, 1970, our 106-year-old house burned. The previous Thanksgiving we were away and someone broke into our tack room and stole our saddles. As a result, Peggy arranged for her secretary to house-sit for the week we were away. The secretary and her friend had a party in the house on Sunday evening. The secretary told the fire chief that as she was preparing to go to work Monday morning, she was smoking a cigarette when the phone rang. She put her cigarette in an ash tray on the arm of an upholstered chair. However, when she got up, she knocked the ash tray between the cushions of the chair. Upon finishing her conversation, she retrieved the ash tray and lit cigarette from the chair, poured a pot of water in the chair, and went to work. She left her friend asleep on the second floor. At ten o'clock, a passing motorist saw flames coming from the windows. He called the fire department. The friend tied bed sheets together and went out the window.

Our next-door neighbor, Dr. Don Enlow, ran into the burning structure to the second floor to be sure our youngest, Tom, was not in his crib. We were visiting Paul and Inta Ertel at their cottage in Pennsylvania at the time. When we got word of the fire, we were told the house was totaled. We headed home.

From the outside, the house didn't look too bad. However, besides the four walls that we had just had rock wool insulation blown into, there was nothing left of the three-storey interior. We could see blue sky, which did not match the gray of our moods. The four-foot diameter electric exhaust fan we had installed on the roof was lying on the cobblestone basement floor.

Marguerite and Bill Oliver opened their home to us for the first two weeks. Then Sue and Morton Cox, who were staying in their cottage at the lake, invited us to move into their city house. Dr. Cox was the ophthalmologist who had repaired my retina two years before. We stayed there until approximately the first of September.

During that time, a grade-school boy who lived behind and beside the Cox home came down with encephalitis—a brain infection. One to two weeks later, our daughter Millie had a similar infection. Both children were hospitalized and went into comas. Dr. Bill Oliver was Millie's pediatrician. Millie came out of her coma, and we proceeded to St. Louis.

One to two months before the fire, Peggy had left the University of Michigan Student Health Service to join the Chelsea Medical Clinic.

At length, we decided to join Masters and Johnson.

In preparation to leave our home, I took Chrissie with me to the burned-out house. Millie was still in the hospital. I took up the one-inch floorboards of alternating white oak and black walnut in the front hall and dining room. Chrissie fell asleep in a smoky, stuffed chair in the dining room. It was hot that August day. It was not a happy day. In a corner of the dining room stood the built-in china cabinet just completed by Mr. Bailey except for the stain and glass. It represented all the work we had put into the house for six years. Then there was Millie in the hospital with encephalitis, from which she might have severe residual. And here I was in our burned-out house, trying to salvage some beautiful flooring.

We locked our farm tractor in the garage with the flooring, packed our two cars, and took our baby-sitter with us to St. Louis. We reported to Dr. Masters on September 1. At our request, they had rented a furnished house for us. In my pocket was the name and number of a pediatric neurologist in St. Louis to monitor Millie's further recovery.

While we were in St. Louis, someone broke into our garage and stole the flooring and the tractor.

Our Work with Masters and Johnson

In addition to treating patients, part of my responsibility was to develop a curriculum with Ms. Virginia Johnson to teach other professionals to do their type of work. Ms. Johnson and I completed the teaching curriculum. Six pairs of therapists took our training course. Peggy was responsible for the operation of the Masters and Johnson infertility clinic. We thought perhaps we would stay with Masters and Johnson indefinitely, so we bought a house. We were with Masters and Johnson two years, September 1970 to September 1972.

Leaving Masters and Johnson

There were several reasons we left Masters and Johnson. We were working five to seven days a week. Patients came to St. Louis for only two weeks. If each of our cases was progressing well, we would not need to go in on Saturday or Sunday; however, that decision could not be made until the day before. After the two weeks, we had scheduled follow-up phone calls with the patients as long as needed. Further, between the two of us, we had five sets of patients at any given time. The chances that all of them would be doing well enough on the same weekend not to need to be seen were slim. Further, vacation time with Masters and Johnson was two weeks at Christmas and two weeks in May for medical meetings. This left no time to travel with our children. Our horses were several miles away, rather than just outside our door where Peggy could see, pet, and talk to them.

The replacement value of the burned house was much more than the insurance company would allow us for the loss, per se. That is, the replacement value was $25,000 more than the estimated market value. We rebuilt the house on the site of the fire. We could sell it, lease it, or move into it. We knew our old jobs were available for us. Our live-in babysitter was eager to return to Michigan.

Newspaper Column

On our return to Michigan, Peggy went to work as a member of the Chelsea Medical Clinic. I opened a private psychiatric practice specializing in sexual dysfunction. Together we saw some couples a la Masters and Johnson. I started teaching sex education at the University of Michigan's Graduate School of Social Work. Also, we were contacted by Ms. Journey of the daily newspaper the *Detroit Free Press* to write a sex-help column for the Knight-

Ridder wire service, which was published one to three times a week from 1973 to 1996.

Our Kids Need Self-Defense

In the second grade, our son, Tom, was being pushed around on the playground. He asked me how to deal with it. I recalled the other kids' reaction when I followed my father's advice. I called the assistant principal and told him what was happening and who was doing it. I expected he would keep his eye peeled for any such actions, then intervene. Months went by; then Tom came to me again. The hazing and physical teasing was worse than before. The assistant principal had called the culprit in and chastised him. Now Tom was being called names like "squealer." I vetoed the first three moves that came to my mind as being too severe. Then I showed Tom my fourth thought: a move that would put the other boy on his back with Tom standing over him, holding and twisting one of his arms. We practiced those moves on each other until Tom was confident and able to execute them very well. He did so. That ended the taunting.

Karate Master

In the late '70s, Millie and Tom asked to take karate lessons. I located a great teacher, Master Edward Sell. He had served in Korea as an MP. While in the U.S. Army he learned karate. At first, Chrissie and I just watched. Then I signed up; it had been boring just watching, and it was an activity I could do with my kids. After another month of watching, Chrissie joined the class. We stopped shortly after Master Sell sold his studio and moved to Florida. All three of my kids had earned brown belts. Just before he left I earned my black belt at age 49. Had Master Sell remained teaching, I would have continued to work with him. I enjoyed the workouts. It was good exercise.

Firearms Education

I taught all three of my children to shoot a rifle, and taught them that every gun is *always* to be considered loaded.

Saving a Man's Life

One sunny afternoon in the summer, I was in the yard when I heard a woman calling, "Help! Help!" Both of my neighbors and I responded. The young woman was telling her boyfriend that she was breaking up with him. He was threatening to throw himself in front of a car. The speed limit was 45, and 50-55 was not an unusual speed. I put the man on his back on the ground, and my 280 to 300-pound neighbor, Mr. Bud Putman, sat on him until the police arrived.

In Good Hands

One day a woman made an appointment with my secretary. The intake sheet indicated she was a minister and was struggling with a very serious decision. At her appointment she came in with her husband. This usually was an indication of a marital problem with the spouse agreeing to come reluctantly. She indicated she was having trouble getting started talking due to the gravity of the issue. To help her, I guessed by asking if she was right with her husband.

She replied, "Oh, yes."

Then I asked if she was right with her children.

Again she said, "Yes."

I asked if she was right with God.

Again she said, "Yes."

I then asked, "What else is there?"

The couple looked at each other, and he said, "I think you are in good hands."

She said, "I think so, too."

Whereupon he got up and left.

Her treatment was successful.

Peggy's Wisdom Prevents Possible Blackmail

In the years Peggy and I were publishing a sex column in the local newspaper, the *Detroit Free Press*, Peggy usually went to bed an hour or so before I did. One night between 11:00 and 11:30, there was a knock on the door. It was a woman, probably in her thirties. Nothing about her stood out to me. She said her car had broken down in front of our house and she needed a ride home. She lived 10-12 miles away. I told her I would take her home as soon as I told my wife.

I woke Peggy and told her what was happening. Half asleep, she said, "I'm going with you." I said there is no need for that. She reiterated that she was going. Again I said that was not necessary, but if she wanted to, okay. She got dressed while I went in to tell our teenage daughter what was happening.

Somehow I had our pickup truck rather than the car we normally used. The stranger sat between Peggy and me. As I got closer to her house, she seemed to become more agitated, not more relaxed, as one would expect.

As we neared her home, her agitation increased. She said I didn't need to take her up to her door. I said that's no trouble, and I need somewhere to turn around. Her voice changed, more anxious and bossy. "You can let me off in the road." It was a dirt road. I said, "Okay, I'll just watch to be sure you get in and get the light on." In a pleading voice, she said, "Don't do it; let me out on the road and just go." I did. I was impressed by Peggy's wisdom. To my mind, she had prevented an accusation of my sexually molesting the woman, and possibly attempted blackmail.

My Mother's Demise

My mother showed signs of dementia at about age 75, just as her mother and her sister had. We all realized that Mother's ability to continue to live independently was greatly limited. Mother did, too, and agreed to sell her home.

By age 85, my mother, as well as her sister, had become psychotic, not knowing even their own names. My aunt was placed in Bethea Baptist Nursing Home in Florence, South Carolina. About 1985, we placed Mother there, also. She died there in 1991 of Alzheimer's Disease. A brain autopsy showed Alzheimer's tangles and multiple small strokes.

Discovering Joseph Campbell

From 1973 to 1979, I read many books by Joseph Campbell, starting with *The Power of Myth*.[12] Joseph Campbell could rightly be called Mr. Mythology. The individual stories and accounts were like other ethnographic accounts, but by gaining some distance from all the details, I got a new and distant perspective.

All societies have myths/stories; they all have powerful figures. They may be helpful, or maleficent, or random erratic mischief-makers by their actions. Their single most predominant feature seems to be their extraordinary power(s).

Is there a human need for someone or something greater than most men? Or perhaps the idea comes from a feeling of inadequacy, of *Can I measure up?* I know that *I am not the strongest or wisest man around.* Could there be a second dynamic?

I also read Huston Smith. I empathized with him in his quest through the world's religions. His writing rationally expressed my thoughts from my teenage years forward.   On a personal or individual level, there seemed to be many places in which God might have intervened, as well as on a national/international level, such as the Holocaust.

My Greatest Regret

About 1979 or '80, I became quite interested in a business venture. I saw it as a two- to three-year commitment before selling out, or as a way to devote half a day a week to generate a stream of income—then I could devote the time to my religious interests—my bliss.

Although there were some warning signs from near the beginning, I persisted. I thought it was a great product and concept, and I liked our president. He had some personality traits that were similar to those of my father. That should have been a major red flag, but I missed it. Our president needed to control. As time went by, it became clear he was using the company position to compensate for some felt inferiority. The company was just getting by. Periodically, the three of us would lend the company money. One deal with $100,000 earnest money was blown because our president insisted on talking to our partner's client twice. Our partner saw this as controlling, so he walked away from further involvement with us.

Two men offered to try to take the company public. Our president rejected even considering this idea.

Secondary to this stress and that of my practice, I had put on 35 pounds. All of this contributed to my need for cardiac surgery in 1997.

I had failed to ask myself often enough, "Am I on the road I want to be on?" This would imply considering other roads. I did recognize I was not in the position I wished to be; I didn't really consciously compare that path with the path of my religious bliss. I failed to "follow my bliss" straightaway, as Joseph Campbell advises in his books, warning against being side-tracked. Instead, I went for money to be able to follow my bliss.

The other question that would have helped me had I asked myself was, "Do you really think that you have enough clout to change this situation?" That would have resulted in a resounding, "No."

These largely wasted years comprise my greatest regrets in life.

Dr. Phifer

During the last years of my psychiatric practice, I had two patients who, independently of each other, brought me printed copies of sermons by Reverend Kenneth Phifer, Senior Minister of the Unitarian Universalist Church of Ann Arbor. I was impressed by the clarity of his thought. I was also impressed by the fact that he would put copies of his sermons in the church foyer, free to anyone who wanted one. This meant two important things to me: First, he was serious about his teaching. Second, he was not afraid to go on record and be vulnerable to criticism.

Heart Surgery

In the late fall of 1996, I was warned that I was in danger of a major heart attack. I had partial occluded arteries and a leaking aortic heart valve, so I was advised to reduce stress, take off weight, and exercise more. About thirty percent of the blood my heart pumped would flow backward to be pumped forward again. Either condition could worsen and require surgery. Surgery would address both problems. Intractable angina triggered the surgery in March 1997, which included the five bypasses and the artificial graphite aortic valve. Unfortunately, when the clamp was re-moved from the aorta, I had a shower of emboli (strokes) to the frontal and temporal lobes of my brain. I was told I would be back to normal in a year. I lacked mental clarity for two years, and have never fully recovered my prior mental abilities.

Peggy had our daughter, Millie, stay with me for three weeks; then my sister Sallie stayed with me for a week. I don't recall either of them being here or with me. I was on a medicine to prevent seizures. When this medication was stopped, I began to regain some memory.

Contemplating Suicide

I don't think I was psychotic, at least not the entire time. I had some insights I knew were crazy. I have wanted never to be a burden to anyone, especially my family. I held on to the hope of improvement. I had "always thought" that to prevent myself from becoming a burden, I would commit suicide. As I contemplated killing myself, I realized that I was too out of it (crazy) to do so. I was incapable of planning and carrying out such an act. Several other considerations blocked some paths. I had donated my body to the Anatomy Department at the University of Michigan, hopefully to be used by medical students studying anatomy. It was a way of "giving back." I also like the idea of returning to medical school, "one last time." The department has the right to reject any body donation. To take a shotgun to myself would have resulted in their rejecting my corpse.

There was also the question of where/how to leave my body to be found. Wherever I left it, that area would be emotionally contaminated for my family. That eliminated the barn and house. Poison could be misinterpreted as murder, but a suicide note might take care of that. Carbon dioxide piped inside the truck left by the side of the road would not likely be interpreted as murder, but what about innocent people discovering me?

It also dawned on me that with so many options, I must not want to commit suicide. That was true; only the wish not to be a burden was stronger. I thought of what I had become and of the dynamics involved in every suicide with varying degrees of strength:

The Four Dynamics of Suicide

The first three dynamics of suicide are the desire to die; the desire to live; and the expression of anger to someone or some injustice, none of which I could think of. The fourth is a call for help. I was already receiving all the help that the family and medical community knew how to give. I was grateful.

At length I hit on a different solution: long-term care nursing-home insurance. That would preclude the burden on the family, which was my goal. But who would give me insurance? Nevertheless, I would try.

I approached TIAA-CREF teachers' retirement funds, which had my retirement accounts since I joined the faculty. I was honest on the application. It was accepted. The average length of stay in a nursing home was 5+ years. The premiums would be $56.10 a month. It was a good deal. I signed up. My thoughts of suicide stopped. I felt relieved. I was also being considerate of my family and gaining some time for myself.

Post-op Recovery

During my own post-operative recovery, I had a period of some "amazing insights." I hurried to write them down. I sealed the envelope containing the insights and hid it. I forgot where. Six to twelve months later I was in the backyard and saw our aluminum square-bow boat upside down to keep rainwater out. Synapses clicked in my brain. Is this where I hid those insights? Under the boat was an envelope. Excitedly I opened it. The writing was gibberish.

For the first 1½ years after surgery, I had a hard time turning off my mind. I recalled the Buddhist techniques for emptying the mind, which I had learned in 1959-60. I employed them. They were effective. I also used the three vowel sounds ah, ou, mu. They, too, were effective.

Becoming a Study Subject

A nurse, Jean Vargas, who had worked with Peggy and worked with closed-head injury patients, told me that the brain continues to recover for seven years after an insult, not just one year.

Some time in this period Terry Tice visited me. He introduced me to Amy Ai, PhD. She was living in his house as a tenant. She had been a physician in China before the Cultural Revolution. On coming to our country she earned a doctorate in social work. She studied the recuperation of patients who had had cardiac surgery.

I became a study subject. Amy and I got along well. I made a suggestion or two. I don't remember when I became a consultant to Amy and then a co-author. We have several publications. The most significant finding is probably "Prayer and Reverence in Naturalistic, Aesthetic, and Socio-moral Contexts Predicted Fewer Complications Following Coronary Artery Bypass."

Prayer As a Variable in Recovery After Cardiac Surgery

This prospective study done with Amy explored prayer, reverence, and other aspects of faith in postoperative complications and hospital length of stay of patients undergoing coronary artery bypass graft surgery. Along with traditional religiousness measures, we examined the sense of reverence in religious and secular contexts. Face-to-face interviews were conducted with 177 patients 2 weeks before surgery at a medical center. Medical variables were retrieved from the national Society of Thoracic Surgeons' Database. Logistic and multiple regression models were performed to predict outcomes. We found that frequent Prayer was associated with reduced complications but not the long duration of hospitalization. Sense of reverence in secular contexts predicted fewer complications and shorter hospitalization. Controlling for complications reduced the initial influence of reverence on hospitalization, suggesting the potential mediation of complications. No interaction between demographics and faith factors was evident. The role of faith in medicine is complex and context-dependent. Future studies are needed on mediating factors.

Exercising With Teaching DVDs

I took off more weight and exercised on a treadmill. Finding the exercise boring, I discovered educational tapes by outstanding professors published by the Teaching Company of Chantilly, Virginia. Most of the tapes I watched were on religious subjects, especially world religions, including those of ancient and primitive societies.

Unitarian Universalism

In January 1999, when I thought I had improved enough to be able to carry on a conversation without grossly embarrassing myself, my wife and I visited the Unitarian Universalist Church where Rev. Ken Phifer was senior minister. The poem *Abou Ben Adhem* has expressed my philosophy and religious attitude since I was a young teenager. The Unitarian Universalist denomination meshes extremely well with my views and those found in the poem. I have found a religious and spiritual home with them. Consider their precepts found in the statement of Principles and Purposes of the By-laws of the Unitarian Universalist Association:

> "We, the member congregations of the Unitarian Universalist Association, covenant to affirm and promote: The inherent worth and dignity of every person; Justice, equity, and compassion in human relations; Acceptance of one another and encouragement to spiritual growth in our congregations; A free and responsible search for truth and meaning; The right of conscience and the use of the democratic process within our congregations and in society at large; The goal of world community with peace, liberty, and justice for all; Respect for the interdependent web of all existence of which we are a part.

> "The living tradition we share draws from many sources: Direct experience of that transcending mystery and wonder, affirmed in all cultures, which moves us to a renewal of the spirit and an openness to the forces that create and uphold life; Words and deeds of prophetic women and men which challenge us to confront powers and structures of evil with justice, compassion, and the transforming power of love; Wisdom from the world's religions which inspires us in our ethical and spiritual life; Jewish and Christian teachings which call us to respond to God's love by loving our neighbors as ourselves; Humanist teachings which counsel us to

heed the guidance of reason and the results of science, and warn us against idolatries of the mind and spirit.

"Grateful for the religious pluralism which enriches and ennobles our faith, we are inspired to deepen our understanding and expand our vision. As free congregations we enter into this covenant, promising to one another our mutual trust and support."

The Ann Arbor congregation, along with many others, has the practice of encouraging every 13- or 14-year-old as well as every member of the congregation to write his or her own credo. Each teen has a mentor and also meets with one of the ministers several times.

The congregation is a "welcoming community." This includes lesbians, gay males, bisexuals, and transgender persons. Everyone is welcome.

There is no need to be concerned about inadvertently offending or hurting someone because of an expressed belief. Acceptance of others' views is assured.

Unitarianism began in the 16thcentury when Michael Servetus of Spain, on reading the *Bible*, did not find any reference to the Trinity. He pushed this idea of one God, Unitarianism. John Calvin had Servetus burned at the stake for this heresy.

King John Sigismund of Transylvania (now part of Romania) issued the "Act of Religious Tolerance and Freedom of Conscience."

"...He affirms that in every place the preachers shall preach and explain the Gospel each according to his understanding of it, and if the congregation likes it, well, if not, no one shall compel them for

their souls would not be satisfied, but they shall be
permitted to keep a preacher whose teaching they
approve. Therefore none of the superintendents or
others shall abuse the preachers, no one shall be re-
viled for his religion by anyone, according to the
previous statutes, and it is not permitted that anyone should threaten anyone else by imprisonment
or by removal from his post for his teaching, for
faith is the gift of God, this comes from hearing,
which hearing is by the word of God."

In the 16th century Francis David wrote, "We do not have to
think alike, to love alike."

Primarily in response to the Calvinistic doctrine of predestination, the Universalists believed that God's love was so great that
ultimately everyone would be saved.

In 1805, one Universalist clergyman, Hosea Ballou, in *A Treatise on Atonement* stated that he believed that "the divine grace of
reconciliation may be communicated to those who have never
been privileged with the volume of divine revelation, and who
have never heard the name of a Mediator proclaimed, as the only
way of life and salvation."[13] This statement speaks to those two
questions that I asked since my teen years.

In 1961, the Unitarians and the Universalists, merged.

These dominations have kept their traditions current.

There are other writings in the history of Unitarian Universalism that have impressed me. Two months after we joined the
church, I signed up for a course taught by Ken Phifer and David
Hall based on the book *The Sacred Depths of Nature*[14] by Ursula
Goodenough. In June, my wife and I took a course on the history
of the denomination. One of the activities of that course was a
sentence-completion section. We were asked to sit beside someone we didn't know. I crossed the room and sat. The first or

second sentence was: "After you die, you ____." I wrote "are dead." The man sitting next to me said, "I wrote the same thing." That man, Chuck Kramer, MD, was also a psychiatrist. He and I became close friends. We had lunch together every week or so. We both joined the same men's group that formed that fall. I think it was Chuck's influence that resulted in my being appointed to chair a committee to develop a curriculum for the program "Initiation of Boys into Manhood."

I did a comprehensive survey of the current and classical literature on the topic. That program was successful; then it was combined with "Coming of Age," a coed program.

Association with Muslims and Others

After 9/11, the Islamic Center of Ann Arbor held an open house. Our whole congregation was invited. About one-hundred members of our church attended. I was one of them. There I met Mohammad Al-Zemm, MD, originally from Syria. He is a radiologist. About a week later, I invited him for coffee. We got along well. For the next year we occasionally had dinner at each other's homes with other guests included. Our minister, Rev. Ken Phifer, was a regular. Then Mohammad and I organized a men's group, half Muslim members and half Unitarian Universalist members. We met twice a month for four years.

The Muslims' biggest difficulty in understanding us seemed to be, "How can you teach your children and youth morality without the concepts of heaven and hell?"

On the other side, the Unitarian Universalists had difficulty understanding how the Muslims living in America could buy cars and houses without paying any interest, which was forbidden by the *Qur'an*. We learned that the parties used a financial calculator to calculate the future value, which included interest. This figure became the amount of the loan. Then they paid that balance down, technically not paying any interest.

The other concept that I and some others had some difficulty understanding was the Muslim belief in Allah's will. In essence we came to understand that humans were to do all they could to bring their desired event about. If that result did not occur, then it was Allah's will. Just before the group disbanded, we Unitarian Universalists learned that one goal of some of the Muslims was to convert us to Islam. They thought it would not be difficult since the Unitarian Universalists did not hold the concept of the Trinity dear.

Our Self-help Marriage Book

Peggy and I became aware of some people, including some friends, who were having marital problems. That was unsettling. Over the next three years, Peggy and I wrote a self-help book for marriages titled, *Maximizing Happiness Through Intimate Communication*[15]. It helped couples understand their difficulties and what to do about them. That book contains an original formulation by us of how love grows and how it shrinks. We taught a course based on this book for four years at the church, then turned the course over to Michael Rudy, MSW, and Diane Agusta, PhD in psychology.

The Interfaith Round Table

Since 2003, I have attended the Interfaith Round Table of Washtenaw County, chaired by Rev. George Lambrides. There I met most of the clergy of other religions who so graciously have helped me with *Toward Interfaith Harmony*.

Siblings

My siblings have known of my religious views, and some about the basis of my convictions. We don't try to convert one another. About 2004, my sister, Sallie Taylor, told me that I made her very sad. When I expressed surprise and asked her how, she replied that when she got to heaven I would not be there. I thanked her for her love. Nothing else seemed appropriate to say. As I write this, the poem *Abou Ben Adhem* returns to my mind.

In 2007, my siblings and their spouses presented Peggy and me with a statue of Pegasus with a nice, loving write-up. (See Exhibit F.)

In 1998, my sister Jane presented me with a poem she wrote expressing her appreciation for me as her big brother. She titled it "To Marshall." (See Exhibit G.)

Search Committee

I was appointed as a member of the search committee to identify a potential new senior minister to recommend to our congregation. It was quite an honor. We reviewed the resumes of a number of applicants and held hour-and-a-half telephone interviews with thirteen. The committee invited four applicants to visit Ann Arbor for personal interviews and to preach a sermon. However, the committee did not find a match with any applicant. The search was extended another year. Again, that second year we did not identify a candidate to recommend to the church. I resigned from the committee to save an estimated four-hundred hours in order to return to my writing.

I am most pleased with our new minister, Rev. Gail Geisenhainer.

Med School Classmate

I had tried to contact George Campbell, a medical school classmate/roommate, when I got married and one other time years later, but I was unsuccessful. The letters were returned despite my having written "please forward" on the envelope and addressing them to the medical college. However, as part of our 50ᵗʰ class reunion, we were each sent a complete roster with addresses of former classmates.

I wrote George in care of the nursing home listed on the roster. A week or so later, I got a phone call from a woman who said she was George's daughter. She said he was on kidney dialysis and might not want to talk to me, that he was trying to die. She did give me his phone number. She asked me if I had known her mother. I hadn't.

Somehow, Peggy and I had neglected to get a cell phone with country-wide coverage. I went to a motel near the reunion and requested to use a phone for a long-distance call, offering to reimburse the cost. The manager agreed. He could hear my side of the conversation when I called.

I told George that I had written to him twice over the years without getting any response. I asked about visiting him that afternoon. He said, "Let's wait till next time." We both knew there would never be a "next time." I said I was staying over and could visit tomorrow. He said, "Let's put that off till next time." I said, "George, I just want to tell you how much I appreciated and enjoyed your friendship, and I wish you well in everything you want to do, including dying." He thanked me, and we hung up. The hotel manager refused money for that call. Or even to tell me the charges.

At the reunion, I learned that Sy Ameen, MD, also a classmate, had been his best man. I relayed that name and address to his daughter. She thanked me.

Eye Operations

All total, I have had eight eye operations: two to remove the cataract on the right (age 11); one to relieve glaucoma on the right (age 11); one to remove the right eye (age 11); one to remove the cataract on the left (age 35); one to reattach the retina on the left (age 35); and two to further secure the retina on left (age 40 and 46).

Today I have trouble reading the newspaper or phone book without a magnifying glass due to edema of the cornea. I am on hypertonic saline eye-drops in an attempt to reduce the swelling. The risk of surgery is a bleed into the eyeball, which could result in complete or total blindness. The ophthalmologist and I agree that surgery is not worth the risk.

My attitude to all of this is realistic and straightforward. I do not consider myself a victim of fate or any supernatural intervention.

During my period of legal blindness from 1963 to 1968, I continued to work as best I could. I wrote articles and supervised residents. I tried to live a normal, usual life. I did hold my head so close to the typewriter that a key would often hit me on the nostril. During this time, the only thing I could see clearly was my wife's eyes, but only by getting within two inches of them. I called her "blue eyes." When I regained my sight, I dropped that name without making a conscious decision. I plan to take the same attitude again, if necessary.

I have always had great support systems, and I am sure I will this time, too.

Conclusions

As I write this in 2010, I am 77 years old. I have lived longer than each of my grandfathers. However, I don't think their cir-

cumstances apply to me. Grandfather Shearer died in a fit of
verbal anger. My mother's father died during the stress of an air-
raid drill in 1943 in Norfolk, Virginia. Still, I am aware that my
heart could kill me at any time. When I finish writing this piece I
will be ready. Don't misunderstand; I will find a number of other
things to work on when this is finished.

I have lived to be ready to die at any moment. These thoughts
have come to the fore whenever I or the family takes a trip. My
will, records, finances, and other papers are in order. I have
donated my body to the Anatomy Department of the University
of Michigan, hopefully to be used as a cadaver for medical students to study anatomy.

I don't have animosity toward anyone. I don't know when I
learned not to hold a grudge, but it was a good principle to have
lived by.

I have enjoyed people—people in all walks of life, and think I
have had the respect of most of them. I have tried to help my
fellow humans—patients, friends, and fellow seekers of knowledge and truth. My patients have always been in a special category. I feel honored that so many allowed me into their lives, and I
believe I helped most. I am not aware of having done any harm to
any of them.

The biggest mistake I made in life was not asking myself frequently enough: "Am I on the path I want to be on?" Asking this
question every six months or so would have resulted in my invest-
ing more time, thought, and energy in religious issues.

I have enjoyed my friends. They have been very special to me.
Siblings and in-laws are extra special to me. They are a great
source of joy and love. Each one has enriched my life.

The thing that has given me the greatest joy and satisfaction
over the years has been my marriage and, right behind that, our

three children—all so different, taking different paths in life, and all so loving.

Life has been grand. I wouldn't have missed it for the world.

Love is a concept, an abstract concept. We see and recognize the manifestations of love, but not the love, per se. In our bedroom hangs a picture of a mother nursing her infant. The mother and child are gazing into each other's eyes. It depicts a manifestation of love. Hopefully their love will deepen and mature as the child matures into an adult and the mother matures into an elderly woman.

God's love is also an abstract concept, but one that can be experienced—felt—just as human love can.

St. John says, "God is love." Contrary to the rules of grammar and logic, I have inverted that sentence to be "Love is God." That statement is probably as close as I will get in my lifetime to comprehending and understanding God. Like Abou Ben Adhem, if my name is not among those who loved the Lord, "I pray thee, then, write me as one that loves his fellow-men."

Acceptance

October 26, 2010

I am of this world.

In this regard, I am like the sands on the beaches. I am like the water in the oceans, the stone of the mountains. We are all subject to the laws of nature. I am no exception.

I am also mortal and subject to the laws of all things mortal. We all die. Death may come as a pounce, or it may creep up on us. We are not constructed like the one-horse shay in Longfellow's poem "The Deacon's Masterpiece". It was constructed so that every part would wear out at exactly the same time. We may protest, even move to delay the inevitable with varying degrees of temporary success.

I have two systems that are giving way: my vision and my mental processing. My medical colleagues and I have done all we know how in order to halt their progressions.

I have worn an artificial eye since the age of eleven. My remaining eye has been operated on four times, but they have given me some sight. Before 1968, I couldn't see my children. However, the surgeries have damaged the outer layer of cells that normally take excess fluid out of the cornea.

Now I have edema (swelling) of the cornea. Usually this is corrected by a corneal transplant, but I am on the blood thinner Coumadin to prevent stroke or heart attack caused by clots forming on my graphite heart valve and breaking free. One of the dangers of corneal transplantation is the potential of a bleed into the eye, which would cause total, permanent blindness. The ophthalmologist says the risk is too great to do the operation. I agree with him for now.

First I lost the ability to read the phone book and road maps, then to read newspapers. I can no longer drive. Although I can see a movie for some distance, I can no longer read the messages on an ATM, a gas pump, or a menu. With the new loss of each capability, I have to struggle with depression. Given the degeneration of my vision, I predict a time when I will only be able to see the sun.

My mental abilities also have been deteriorating. I first noticed an inability to recall some nouns, especially proper nouns, including the names of friends I have known for decades. This has caused some embarrassing pauses. I have lost the ability to do simply math in my head. Peggy has taken over our checkbook. I have long enjoyed a good sense of direction, easily retracing my steps, but during a recent trip with my nephew to the Henry Ford

Museum, I would have needed to ask directions a half-dozen times to find my way back. Both the neurologist and neurosurgeon agree that I do not have Alzheimer's. On October 26, I underwent brain surgery to treat communicating hydrocephalus. Only time will tell if that provides relief for my mental condition.

Muslims believe in doing everything possible to create a favorable outcome, but then accepting the inevitable as Allah's will. I do need to accept the inevitable and grieve once for the whole course. I should not let depression dog each step of deterioration and permeate my grief over every noticeable progression.

I can, I *will* enjoy the warm and lusty greetings of family and friends, the shared joys with my children, the laughter of my grandchildren.

I will enjoy my wife's smile, and appreciate her embraces. I will cherish every moment I still might spend with the love of my life.

I accept that I am subject to the laws of nature.

I am of this world.

Exhibit A

Concern About Fairness to Judas Iscariot

By Marshall L. Shearer, M.D.

This subject has been bothering me since my teenage years:

Jesus was on a mission from God. John the Baptist saw Jesus coming toward him, and said, "Behold, the lamb of God, who takes away the sins of the world...." John 1:29

This is repeated the next day. John 1:36.

(The mission had 2 sub-goals. One was to maintain a schedule in regard to Holy Week; the other was to fulfill certain prophecies. Be alert for these factors as you read the scripture.)

"...Jesus began to show his disciples that he must go to Jerusalem and suffer many things from the elders and chief priests and scribes. And be killed, and on the third day be raised." Matthew 16:21-23

"As (Jesus and the disciples) gathered in Galilee, Jesus said to them, 'The son of man is to be delivered into the hands of men, and they will kill him, and he will be raised on the third day.' And they were greatly distressed." Matthew 17:23

"I am not going up to the feast, for my time has not fully come." John 7:8

"...They sought to arrest him, but no one laid a hand on him because his hour had not yet come." John 7:30

"Now as Jesus was going up to Jerusalem, he took the twelve disciples aside and said to them. 'We are going up to Jerusalem, and the Son of Man will be betrayed to the chief of priests and the teachers of the law. They will condemn him to death and will turn him over to the Gentiles to be mocked and flogged and crucified. On the third day he will be raised to life!'" Matthew 20:17-19

"And the chief priests and the scribes were seeking how to put him (Jesus) to death for they feared the people. Then Satan entered into Judas called Iscariot, who was a member of the twelve. He went away and conferred with the chief priest and captains how he might betray him to them. And they were glad and engaged to give him money. So he agreed and sought an opportunity to betray Jesus to them the absence of the multitude." Luke 22:2-6

"Now on the first day of the Unleavened Bread the disciples came to Jesus saying, 'Where will you have us prepare for you to eat the Passover?' He said, 'Go into the city to such a one and say to him: The Teacher says, "My time is at hand; I will keep the Passover at your home with my disciples." And the disciples did as Jesus had directed them, and they prepared the Passover. And when it was evening, he sat at table with the twelve disciples, and as they were eating he said, 'Truly, I say to you, one of you will betray me.' And they were sorrowful, and began to say to him one after another, 'Is it I, Lord?' He answered, 'He who has dipped his hand in the dish with me.' The son of man goes as it is written of him, but woe to that man by whom the son of man is betrayed! It would have been better for him if he had not been born.' Judas who betrayed him, said, 'Is it I, Master?'" And he said to him, 'You have said so.' Matthew 26:17-25

"Jesus said to them (the disciples), 'You will all fall away because of me this night, for it is written "I will strike the shepard and the sheep of the flock will be scattered."'" Matthew 26:31

"Then he (Jesus) said to them, 'My soul is very sorrowful, even unto death and troubled; remain here and watch with me.' And going a little further he fell on his face and prayed, 'My father, if it be possible, let this cup pass from me; nevertheless, not as I will, but as thou wilt.'" Matthew 26:38-39

"Then he came to his disciples and said to them, 'Are you still sleeping and taking your rest? Behold the hour is at hand and the son of man is betrayed into the hands of sinners. Rise, let us be going; see my betrayer is at hand.'

"While he was still speaking, Judas came, one of the twelve, and with him a great crowd with swords and clubs, from the chief priest and the elders of the people. Now the betrayer had given them a sign, saying, 'The one I shall kiss is the man. Seize him.' And he came up to Jesus and said, 'Hail, Master!' And he kissed him. Jesus said to him, 'Friend, why are you here?' Then they came up and laid hands on Jesus and seized him." Matthew 26:45-50

"Do you think that I cannot appeal to my father, and he will at once send me more than twelve legions of angels? But how then should the scriptures be fulfilled, that it must be so?" Matthew 26:53-54

The account in St. John is slightly different: Judas procured a band of soldiers and some officers from the chief priests and the Pharisees, then went there with lanterns and torches and weapons. Then Jesus, knowing all that would happen to him, came forward and said to them, "Whom do you seek?" They answered him, "Jesus of Nazareth." Jesus said to them, "I am he." Judas, who betrayed him, was standing with them when he said to them, "I am he." They drew back and fell to the ground. Again he said to them, "Whom do you seek?" And they said, "Jesus of Nazareth." Jesus answered, "I told you I am he. So if you seek me let these men go." This was to fulfill the word which he had spoken. "Of those you gave me I lost not one." John 18:3-10

Jesus made no attempt to deceive or evade. If Jesus knew this would be the case, then why was Jesus so critical of Judas betraying him? Jesus betrayed himself. As I read St. John scripture, Judas seems more of a facilitator than a betrayer. The men sent to arrest Jesus did not know him. Jesus twice told them who he was. Suppose they had arrested the wrong man? Judas helped keep the happenings on time. Suppose the officials delayed until after the Passover? The officials needed Judas to identify Jesus, and they recognized the fact in agreeing to pay Judas thirty pieces of silver to do so; yet Jesus said it would be better for that man if he had never been born. Judas ignored that statement. I attribute that to the fact that Judas must have thought Jesus would invoke his supernatural powers to intercede. When Judas realized he had misunderstood, he hanged himself. Did he not hear Jesus' rebuke of Peter for saying Jesus should not be killed? What Judas failed to adequately understand was Jesus' mission—that of being an unblemished sacrifice. Jesus had told his disciples of his mission. He knew everything else that was going to happen.

Jesus also said he didn't lose any man that God had given him. Matthew 26:38 Did he not lose Judas? Doesn't Judas count?

The Gospel According to Judas

Around AD 180 Irenaeus, Bishop of Lyon of Roman Gaul, wrote a treatise, "Against Heresies," which denounced, among others, The Gospel According to Judas. The original document was written in Greek; the existent document is in Coptic, the language of Egypt around the early Christian centuries.

The codex was found in 1945 in a jar in the sands of Egypt, near the town of Nag Hammadi. Other writings were found with it. Among them: The Gospels of Thomas, The Gospel of Philip, The Gospel of Truth, and others. The Gospel of Judas has been carbon dated to between AD 220 and 340. Studies on the ink are consistent with these dates.

The Gospel of Judas remained unread until 1983. It depicts the struggle between the Gnostics and the hierarchical church, which endorses only the Gospels of Matthew, Mark, Luke, and John.

The document describes a special relationship between Jesus and Judas and their secret conversations. Judas is depicted as the only disciple who truly understands Christ's message. He is depicted as doing his leader's bidding in handing Jesus over to the Roman authorities. Supposedly, Jesus tells Judas, "You will be sacrificing the man that physically clothes me," thereby getting rid of Jesus' physical body. This is depicted as a favor to Jesus. Jesus also tells Judas, "You will be cursed for it."

SOURCE: Archives of the National Geographic Society, May 2006, which was agreed to between the Society and Egyptian authorities. The originals were to be returned to Egypt, and the Society was to hold the rights to the translation and the media rights.

COMMENT: I have little doubt that Judas felt and believed he had a special relationship with Jesus. Jesus was charismatic. I expect he could and often did engender feelings of special closeness in others. Even today in 2010, there are people who feel-believe that they have a special relation with Jesus. However, Judas was not among the three disciples that Jesus asked to accompany him to pray in Gethsemane. Mark 14:32-33

Criteria for judging the truth of accounts such as this one are its reasonableness and how well the new story fits or modifies the older one(s). Jesus had told his disciples that he must go to Jerusalem and be crucified. Therefore, there was no need for secrecy. The disciples had been informed. It was important that Jesus be killed as a sacrifice.

Why did Judas hang himself? The only aspect of these happenings that Judas might have miscalculated is that Jesus would not ask his father for help, or that God would intervene without Jesus asking. Jesus was likely aware of Psalms 91, which says that God would help him. I think Judas expected Jesus to ask for help, thereby establishing Jesus' kingdom on earth as a consequence. I expect that in Judas' mind the establishment of the kingdom would negate Jesus' statement of "it would be better for that men had he never been born."

Jesus did give his disciples one more commandment: "Love one another." John 16:33

Exhibit B

Of God and Santa Clause

By Marshall L. Shearer, M.D.

Science has vanquished mankind's notion of the universe as his egotistical domain, and is forcing him to ponder his status anew. Perhaps man is not the purpose of all creation. Perhaps he is not the central figure in all existence. Could it be that man is as insignificant as an ant in the cosmos? Man has lost his God, lost his fairy angel. He is no longer the favorite of the favorite. He has lost his protector. He stands as an orphan in the universe.

But has he really lost it? Or has he only grown out of the delusion? Oh, the pain of the loss is no less, but the prognosis is much better.

Man now stands as a child of five or six years of age, who over a period of one or two years has contemplated Santa Clause. He has heard people say there is such a man; others say there is not. He has seen the acts attributed to Santa Clause, and they are good. He hates the thought of their loss, but reason tells him that a fat jolly man cannot get down a six-inch stove pipe, that the house is locked tightly each night, that reindeer cannot fly, that it would be impossible for one person to deliver presents to everyone in the same night. The realization that the jolly fat man in the red suit is a myth comes slowly, mournfully…and when it is complete, he has lost a dear friend. He has lost an incentive to be good, to avoid wrong. He stands still, hands in pockets, eyes on the ground, and takes a deep breath as he shakes his head slowly from side to side. He is growing up. He is as yet too young to comprehend the spirit of unselfishness, of giving, of sharing. He looks on the stuffed stocking as a duty of his parents—something taken for granted.

When he is a little older, he will recognize the greatness of Santa Clause. The unselfish act to bring another joy is to say, "Your life means something to me; this is a token of my esteem for you. I do not have to do this, but because of my recognition of your beneficial influence on my life, I make this gesture." But can a child of five or six comprehend such a love gift? Or understand that Santa Clause is really the spirit of demonstrating appreciation and love?

With mixed emotions, the child realizes there is no fat man at the North Pole with books to keep on one's goodness and badness, no army of elves to spy on one, no dutiful payday once a year. Today mankind has lost his God; his omnipotent, omniscient, and omnipresent God; his Father; his benefactor; his rewarder and punisher. And with it he has lost his heaven and hell. He is no longer the chosen. The world and universe no longer revolve around him; it is he who is revolving. He, too, has lost an incentive to be good, without a payday at the end of life. He, too, is alone now without heavenly records of his actions, without...without—just plain "without." He, too, stands still, hands in pockets, and looks from the sky to the people around him; he also comes to fix his eyes on the ground with a sigh and a tear in his heart. The people who are still happy in their belief in an anthropomorphic god, he passes, not wishing to force upon them the painful realization he feels.

He counts the loss. The wars...the religious wars, the worship, the subservience, the sacrifice, the time, the money, the thought, the energy... "Good God" the *loss*. He fears a loss of ethics, too. But how many boys were good because of Santa Clause? How many men because of heaven and hell?

Man now has to realize the other implications of his new awareness: the freedom to build a more stately mansion for his soul; the loss of religious prejudice (not mere toleration); freedom of thought; and the ability to discuss freely and rationally, to study, to be…himself. The added leisure afforded by the loss of uncertainty (uncertainty as to whether a sick wife or child will recover)…all's dead now. Now he can turn to new horizons, and like the man who lost his dear wife, he is without direction, devotion, or orientation…and for a while he will drift. Then lacking anywhere else to turn, he will eventually turn to himself. And there, hidden deep within the cloistered recesses of his being, he will find the spiritual essence of himself, his lost god.

It was hard to accept Santa Clause as a spiritual being within the human heart. It was easier to personify that being and project him into the world of place and flesh—a jolly fat man at the North Pole. It will be much harder for man to come to accept and appreciate God as a spiritual being within himself rather than a king-judge dressed in white robes sitting on a throne in a place called heaven.

As man grows, he will slowly come to realize that the messages of all the other benefactors of mankind were distortions by those who heard and recorded them. The distortions were due to their own myopia, by their own limitations and convictions, regardless of their integrity and attempts at honesty. They were inspired by the message they heard, and they recorded it in their own language, the language of their time, metaphors, expectations, and unquestioned assumptions.

Man will gradually come to see through the mirror less dimly, come face to face with the vision that Christ and all the other benefactors were upholding: the unselfishness in thought, in feeling, in action—unselfishness in love that is the true spirit of the Holy Ghost, the image of God in man. He will come to realize salvation is not for the taking, but for the giving of the love gift, the self. It is not something dead, but alive, living in the here and now of today and tomorrow, something capable of growth, something to mature. It is not something to be received on payday, something selfish in itself, but a release from selfishness. It is not what or who loves man, but what and whom man loves. It is a sense of humbleness, a willingness to forgive one's self, and hence the ability to forgive others, shortcomings. It is a sense of others, a growing, ever-growing, widening and enriching love, a love potentially as total and consuming as that of Jesus.

Mankind will slowly come to find the abode of his lost god, not far off and out of reach, but within himself—the spirit of compassion, of benevolence, of friendship, of love—the true term for the Holy Ghost, the image of God in Man—the Incarnate Image of God manifest.

"Thank thee, God, for the concrete image of thee, when I had need of them as a child. Thank Thee more that I can put away childish things and see Thee as a man. Give me, I pray, the ability to act as a man in a more mature image of Thee, in the image of Love. Thank Thee, God, for Santa Clause."

Exhibit C

Poem

By Marshall Shearer (Jr.)

My god is slain;
My love is lost.
My goal is dead,
My life extent.

I have no master
except dejection,
No love aside de-
pression,
No occupation
but reflection.

My only wish—
emancipation.

9/5/57

Exhibit D

To My Mother On Her Sixtieth Birthday

By Marshall Shearer (Jr.)
February 2, 1960

To the one who nursed and changed me,
Dressed and bathed me,
Rocked and lulled me;
To the one who loved me first;
To the one who gave me birth;

To the one who held and sang me,
Cheered and mused me,
Spanked and trained me;
To the one who held me close;
To the one I love the most;

To my mother who helped me with my work,
Who listened to my troubles,
Who smiled at my tales,
And recoiled from my frogs;
To the greatest love I ever knew;

To my mother who forced not her God upon me,
Who tolerated all my insurrections,
Who sent me forth with a mother's blessing;

To my mother who cherished every dream I cherished,
Who cried every tear I shed,
I thank you for your love
So beautiful, rich and free;

And to the heavenly god(s) above,
I thank Thee for that love
My mother gave to me.

Exhibit E

My Father Has Embarked

By Marshall L. Shearer, M.D.

It is a hot, humid afternoon in May, 1964, that we bury my daddy on a grassy knoll in North Carolina. Atop the knoll six enlisted men in fresh whites fire a three-gun salute. Heavy hangs the thick stillness; then the lone bugle's call steals through the stolid stillness of the air. "Gone is the sun from the lakes, from the hills, from the sky…all is well…safely rest…God is nigh."

Its message is clear: Gone…gone…gone from this clay the soul that lives; from this brow, the furrows that care; from these lips the love and laughter…. Gone…looted clean of its clay the man who was…. Gone…gone. Only the empty tomb remains. The stillness hangs without support.

"All is well"…small consolation. The stillness mounts…but all is well with him. 'Tis I, I and those about me who hurt…all is well with him. There *is* some consolation….

"Safely rest"…breathing is easier somehow, the stillness less heavy. Safely rest…the last deed is done, the last word is said…and nothing was left undone or unsaid between us. We filled the minutes of the years with 60 seconds full of distance run. There are no candles to light, no prayers needed to lift his soul. He lived right mightily. All is still, as motionless as that giving heart and noble chest. In that stillness all has become one…inseparable… "God is nigh"…. Where? They both are gone! Where? Cast about. There at my left side is my mother. Here at my side is my mother…. Here at her side am I. In the sobs and the stillness all has been one. We each reach to pat the other's hand. Here is love, God is nigh. I gaze over my shoulder. Through the brine of my eyes I see…. I find *Him* again in the oneness of that sea of tears with its rolling, sobbing crests. The hillside is flooded. The tide is at its flood. My father has embarked.

The commander is presenting my mother with our nation's flag. Sunglasses hide his eyes. He says something about my father's service to his country. *He* doesn't know! I guess the uniform does…that's the wrong flag. It's only the Stars and Stripes. It should be white with a red cross on a blue field. "Thank thee, God, for sparing him during the war, for saving him from those torpedoes and bringing him to me…to us. Thank thee, God, for sparing him in 1956…the railroad tracks were lonely that night…I had trouble finding You that night, too. You seemed to have retreated to the stars. Somehow I reached you there; many others reached you, too. He wasn't gone then; You spared him for us. Thank thee, God…. And I guess I never thanked You for sparing him from his first heart attack in '57. Thank thee, God, for such parents. Be with Mother, and Sallie and Robert and Jane, and comfort them…and all the others in that sea of tears. Uncle, leaning against that post, looked like he could use some—and TT and Lanny and Uncle Dave and his brothers, Uncle Al and Uncle Bob, and all the rest…. The tide has turned…it's ebbing now. The sea will cast many, many torn fragments and much frothy brine in his memory ere the wound heals and the waves beat the rough coast smooth again. My father has embarked.

Back to the bosom and womb of Mother Nature and the earth go the salts. He loved the red clay that holds him. He is gone. But I must come again to this spot for three more plantings. How sacred can one piece of sod be? I have met the first. God give me strength. Thank thee, God, for a little while…for moments to fill with joy and happiness and love with them for a little while—moments I can no longer fill for him. My father has embarked.

The flowers overflow the grave. They bloom for a season, and they, too, will die and be no more. What has the mind and hand of God wrought? An endless procession of endings. I know not what lies beyond the stillness of life. As the unborn babe, I cannot see, nor can I imagine existence outside the confines of the womb. It matters not. The earth is my womb, is my existence now. And here in my world I feel and see an immortality to rival the heavens of the ancients. There is a void inside me now because it once was filled. The sides of that void bear the mark of its mold…are its template…more indelible than if cut by sculptor's chisel in granite. How many voids did his soul leave? How big? How many souls bear his mark? The flowers overflow the grave…twice overflow. As will be all human voids, they are first filled with an oceanic brine, and slowly over seeming eons the void today full with salty tears will be refilled with soul stuff. In each of us the template on the edges of the void formed, fashioned, and tempered in the meaningful moments of life when our two souls came naked face to face and burned its mark each on the other in a fission of radiance. That soul is no longer in juxtaposition, no longer available to flash and sparkle and radiate and mirror the image of God in man. It is gone…gone wherever souls go. But it has burned a parcel of its form on each of us who knew it. The template is true. Now we must grow…replace the briny void with a finer soul—larger, grander, better cut, better able to radiate love, God's essence, on to other souls. More in death than in life will we imitate him as we expand to fill that void and make that which was once on our surfaces, deep within as part of us. On down through the eons of time will that soul form, burned into him by those he knew, burned into others by those who knew him…. My father has embarked.

What is that form that was him…that in part is to become more a part of me?

It seems I always saw the pride, the pride of a job well done, of honesty, of a family name, of a man to be counted, of openness and frankness, of bravery and valor—the pride of industry and of duty well-performed.

I always saw the dreams of mountains to climb, of things to do, the dreams made of ambitions for self or others.

It seems I always saw the wisdom in those blue eyes and curly locks, respected and sought by many far and near. I always saw fairness.

I always saw the interest in others, the giving, the unselfishness, the devotion, the love.

Long it seems I've been aware of the curious mixture of willingness to take a stand and steadfastness once the course is set, with insecurity, doubt, and inferiority between the dream and the set of the course. At times, with a self-defeating sense of unworthiness to cross the goal and grasp the prize, he faltered when, but for the closing of his hand, it was his. This my mother could accept within him and love as part of him. The idealism of youth and its despise of weakness had years ago given way to a tolerance, a tolerance which at times I begrudgingly grant myself when I sense that same inferiority. But in him, my tolerance had given way to a growing acceptance.

The pride, the dreams, the wisdom, the fairness, the love, and that added mixture of steadfastness and faltering, these have I long known, and I thought I knew my father exceedingly well. But I have been blind to one major—perhaps his greatest—facet, a facet I have often wished for myself and at times prayed for in my own way, a facet which I must have confused with inferiority to be blind to it so long, a facet which makes a curious mixture with pride; but even now I am not sure he was aware of it. It was so natural for him. There was no pride in it as there was in other virtuous facets. And indeed, there could not be. That major facet was humility, humbleness with man as well as God.

The preacher opened the service with Tennyson's "Crossing The Bar." It was a poor reading. The punctuation was largely ignored and sprinkled in, some words mispronounced. There was no eloquence. He, as a new minister, there about eight weeks, knew my father but little. He could not have felt much personal loss, though undoubtedly moved by the congregation's tone. My first thought, as usual, was critical. Then it came across my mind like a clarion bell that this was the way he would have wanted it. He chose this church. He knew the people and the type of minister they would have, yet he worshiped there many, many years. My father's diction and rhetoric was more polished than mine, and yet had "Crossing The Bar" been read other than as it was, it would not have been his church. Who is this man who chooses to pray here?—to pray, to teach, to labor and worship, and yet never say a word about all my indictives and murmurings in all these years? There were no hysterics, no great sobs, but everyone in that packed house had trouble breathing. Not an eye was dry; the men seemed unaware of the tears on their cheeks. There were many a bitten lip. There seemed to be more men than women there…. Funerals are for the living, not the dead.

If the Charleston service was simple and plain, the North Carolina internment was simpler. My sister called it "hicky." Two more scripture verses and Christ would have raised Lazarus from the dead. The Sunday service was also hicky. These people were simple folk…but they loved. My father knew them. He knew the general tone of his internment, yet he chose it over Arlington National Cemetery or anywhere else. It was the way he wanted it.

Whence came this humility? The stories told about his athletic career, his work in oil fields…challenging men to hit him in the chest…are all devoid of humility.

My father chose to be buried next to his wife and father-in-law. Of all traits, humility, genuine humility, radiated in a sunny warmth from his father-in-law. It was in every action, every word, every thought, every feeling. My father told a story about himself and his father-in-law only once: My grandfather had a farm which he rented out. After several years, he had it surveyed. His neighbor had built his house ten feet on Grandfather's land and had taken in the spring. Daddy, who was there, was ready to fight—both legally and physically. My grandfather half-laughingly said, "Well, we won't fall out about it." He went down to the courthouse and for $1.00 deeded the neighbor fifteen feet, including the spring. He never even got the dollar. In recollection, my father told that with some wonderment and admiration in his voice.

Was my father's humility the result of filling a briny void of his father-in-law? Such voids do not only result from death, but from little meaningful absences—maybe the eight-hour work day. Death only makes us acutely aware of them. Not only are they larger, but the soul which once was there in essence is forever gone...gone.

My father has embarked.

The sting of death is said to be sin. That may be so for the dying, but for the living, the sting of death is loneliness. There no longer exists that soul with which my soul kindled fire and mirrored God's love. Gone are my chances to share happiness with him. It was about two hours before the essence of his death struck me.... I will never see my daddy again. He never saw the place we just bought. He would have loved it. He will get no joy from it. Somehow the place is of less value. I was cutting the grass the other day...Daddy will never see these fields trimmed. He will get no joy or pride again from seeing a job well done by his son. I am moved not to cut anymore. The beds we bought when we thought he and mother would be here June 1, the ones we picked out…he will never see, never get to enjoy. As I show friends the place, as they dream with us, I sometimes want to stop. He, the dreamer, never got to dream with us. It is easier to call TT's (my mother's sister's) where my mother is visiting because I don't automatically expect to also talk with my father. That voice I shall never hear again.

My father has embarked.

His race is run, his record made, his last deed is done, and justly can he be proud. He has embarked.

His last dream has been dreamt, his last thought aimed, his last plan drawn. He has embarked.

His last utterance has been made, his last counsel given, his last stand taken, his last doubt doubted. He has embarked.

His last smile has beamed, his last laugh shared, his last amen prayed, his last love given.

He has embarked.

He has embarked. You and I remain. I cannot give or share with him, but somewhere from within that briny void a voice declares: "In as much as you do it for the least of these, my brethren, you do it unto me."

My father has embarked.

June 29, 1964

<u>Exhibit F</u>

To The Doctors Shearer

(Presentation by Siblings and In-laws)

To the Doctors Shearer, siblings, healthcare profession-
als, equine adventurists, and just wonderful caretakers of
our generation of the Shearer Clan. We want to recognize
your enormous contributions to each of us individually and
collectively through the years and have chosen a Pegasus as
a token of our love, esteem, and gratitude.

A simple horse was not enough, noble animal that he
is, because you are anything but simple. To the contrary, we
need to recognize the complexity of your lives, but we knew
we had to have something horsey to find a cozy and promi-
nent place in your home. So we added the grace and vision
of the eagle and all that it, too, represents; not just in the
animal kingdom, but for its symbolism for freedom, cou-
rage, independence, and integrity.

We are inspired by your steadfast support, coaching,
nurturing, and sharing, and could never find any symbol
that rises to the level of our admiration, loyalty, and love,
but we hope that "Pegasus" will be a warm and constant
reminder of your lifetime of accomplished leadership.

Exhibit G

To Marshall

(A poem by Marshall's sister Jane Sharpe)
September 10, 1998

From my earliest memories
Despite distance and time,
I have been anchored
Like a kite in your love.
You've given me things that linger
In me like a song.
You taught me that answerable questions
Are only a starting place
And that it's the unanswerable ones that count.
Your voice has rubbed gently
Inside the chambers of my imagination
With rainbows of ideas.
You have opened to me vast regions
And helped me to soar in ever-widening circles.
Somehow you always had time for me
To explain Hindu philosophy,
To teach me to eat an orange in Spanish,
To rescue me from drowning
Both on the Isle of Palms
And recently in Iceland.
You are a sheltering oak
That protects and refreshes.
All my life,
My soul has walked a step behind yours
With your inner fire drawing me after you
Like the pull of the moon.
With gratitude and love for you,
Precious big brother,
My heart overflows.

End Notes

1. "Abou Ben Adhem" by James Henry Leigh Hunt, *One Hundred and One Famous Poems*, compiled by Roy Cook, p 82, Contemporary Books Inc, Chicago, IL, 1958
2. Carroll, Rev. B. H.: *An Interpretation of the English Bible, The Four Gospels*, pp 345-346, Broadman Press, Nashville, TN, 1913
3. Brown, D. MacKenzie: *Ultimate Concern, Tillich in Dialogue*, p 154, Harper and Row, New York, 1865
4. Kushner, Rabbi Harold: *Why Bad Things Happen to Good People*
5. *Bible*, Leviticus 26:13; Revelation 21:3; Ezekiel 37:27; Jeremiah 7:23 & 30:22
6. Matheson, George: *The Spiritual Development of St. Paul*, E. R. Herrick & Company, Edinburgh, 1890
7. Muesse: Hinduism pp 37 & 50
8. "Invictus" by William Ernest Henley, *One Hundred and One Famous Poems*, compiled by Roy Cook, p 95, Contemporary Books Inc, Chicago, IL, 1958
9. "His Letter" by Robert Service, *The Collected Poems of Robert Service*, Vail-Ballou Press, Inc., Binghamton, NY, 1940
10. Yates, Elizabeth: *Skeezer, Dog with a Mission, A True Account of a Canine Co-therapist Who Helps Emotionally Disturbed Children*, Harvey House Publishers, Irvington-on-Hudson, NY, 1973
11. Shearer & Shearer: *Rapping About Sex*, Harper and Row, 1972
12. Campbell, Joseph: *The Power of Myth*
13. Cassara, Ernest, editor: *Universalism In America, A Documentary History of a Liberal Faith*, Skinner House Books, Boston, 1984; 3rd Edition, 1997
14. Goodenough, Ursula: *The Sacred Depth of Nature*
15. Shearer & Shearer: *Maximizing Happiness Through Intimate Communication*, Xlibris, 2004; 3rd Edition: Fresh Ink Group, Roanoke, TX, 2011

Relationships
Communication
Spirituality

www.DocShearer.com

Learn more about the Doctors Shearer and their books

Free Memberships!

Receive free essays, stories, and updates
Join our private, no-spam emailing list

www.FreshInkGroup.com

Discover Fresh Ink books, artists, & writers

info@FreshInkGroup.com

Tell us what you think of
My Life and Spiritual Journey

www.ingramcontent.com/pod-product-compliance
Lightning Source LLC
Chambersburg PA
CBHW031319040426
42443CB00005B/143